# What God Did for Me

# *What God Did for Me*

*EDITED BY*
**Mildred F. Stone**

**Rutledge Hill Press**
Nashville, Tennessee 37210

Published in Nashville, Tennessee, by Rutledge Hill Press, Inc., 513 Third Avenue South, Nashville, Tennessee 37210

Typography by ProtoType Graphics, Inc., Nashville, Tennessee

**Library of Congress Cataloging-in-Publication Data**

What God did for me.

   1. Christian biography.   2. Northeastern Bible College (Essex Fells, N.J.)—Alumni—Biography.
I. Stone, Mildred F.
BR1702.W47   1988     248.2′092′2  [B]    88–23941
ISBN 0-93495-93-4

Printed in the United States of America
1 2 3 4 5 6 7 8 9 — 94 93 92 91 90 89 88

# Table of Contents

*Dedicated*

*to*

*Dr. Charles W. Anderson*
*Founder, President, Chancellor*
*Northeastern Bible College*

# Foreword

The authors of the autobiographical chapters of this book were asked to write about their most memorable experiences with God. These men and women are all full-time Christian workers, engaged in a great variety of ministries, literally around the world. They are preachers, teachers, Bible translators, church planters, evangelists, and executives of Christian organizations.

They are also all graduates of what is now the Northeastern Bible College of Essex Fells, New Jersey. Some of them were early students right after it was founded in 1950 as the Northeastern Bible Institute. The graduates are united in testimony to the academic excellence of the college. (It is the only professionally and regionally accredited Bible College in New England, New York, and New Jersey.) They also are united in their appreciation for their personal relationships with the college faculty and staff, a group of caring people. Their concern for students, beyond the call of duty, literally changed lives as young people were preparing for life ministries.

This book reflects how, in memorable experiences, God touched individual lives with guidance, protection, provision, and comfort, all evidences of His love and power.

In the production of the book the volunteer typing help of three friends was most valuable. Barbara Thompson, Margaret Moffett, and Lillian Andrew had previously given volunteer service to Northeastern in various ways and this latest help was again greatly appreciated.

All of us—authors, typists, and editor—are united in the prayerful assurance that this book will be for readers an inspiration and a blessing.

Mildred F. Stone, Editor

# What God Did for Me

**Mitchell L. Glaser**

# ~ 1 ~

# The Forty-seventh Street Massacre

## Mitchell L. Glaser

*Mitchell Glaser is a key assistant to Moishe Rosen, founder and head of Jews for Jesus. He is responsible for recruiting, training, and development of new staff, as well as coordinating new Jews for Jesus chapters in the United States.*

*Growing up in a traditional Jewish home in New York City, he began attending Hebrew school at age eight, studying Jewish culture, history, and religion two hours a day for five days a week. At age thirteen he was bar mitzvahed. After public high school, where he began to be involved with drugs, he entered the University of Bridgeport in Connecticut, but in the spring of 1969 he and his best friend decided to hitchhike to California. They wanted something, but did not know what it was, Glaser says now.*

*In California they met a Jewish girl who became a Christian, as did Glaser's friend. Then Glaser reports: "One day I prayed and asked God to reveal Himself to me. That night I found a New Testament in a phone booth. I was shocked, of course, but not too shocked to keep me from reading the book. . . . In a matter of days I received Jesus as my Savior and Lord. The changes began almost immediately, and by the time I read 2 Corinthians 5:17 for the second time I knew I was a changed man, a new creation in Jesus, the Jewish Messiah."*

*Soon after becoming a Christian, Glaser met Moishe Rosen who encouraged him to go to Northeastern Bible College in Essex Fells, New Jersey. He graduated from there in 1974 and sub-*

13

*sequently attended Talbot Theological Seminary in La Mirada, California. During his days at Talbot he met and married Zhava, a Jewish believer who was also called to serve the Lord in Jewish missions. The Glasers now live in San Francisco and have a baby daughter, Miriam.*

*During his early days with Jews for Jesus, Glaser was a leader of the Liberated Wailing Wall, one of the organization's mobile evangelistic teams. Since 1976 he has traveled extensively overseas, leading teams to Northern Ireland, ministering in Argentina, and conducting a world tour to English-speaking countries including England, South Africa, Hong Kong, and India, as well as Israel.*

*Since 1982 Mr. Glaser has been an active member of the board of governors of Northeastern Bible College.*

---

I heard the screams and the shrieking of whistles and began to run. As soon as I crossed Seventh Avenue, I saw the crowds beginning to form. People were darting out of their stores; and before my eyes, the taunting crowd turned into a hostile mob. The nine of us who had been handing out tracts in the Diamond District of New York City found ourselves surrounded by hundreds of angry Jewish people.

Before I could even utter a prayer for courage, the fists began flying and a young woman to my left was hit in the face. The crowd continued to build and press in on us, shouting, as if intoxicated by rage.

Still a young believer just recently graduated from Northeastern Bible College, I was to begin seminary later that month. However, at that moment, I had serious doubts whether I would ever make it.

Baruch Goldstein, the leader of our team, began hollering, "Police! Police! We're being persecuted because we believe Jesus is the Messiah!" Soon others of us joined in, but I had little hope that the police could get to us in time. The taunting of the crowd increased with every moment. The young and the elderly screamed together, "Nazis! Anti-Semites!" The physical abuse paled in light of the emotional attack because I felt as though my "enemies" were members of my own family!

The attackers didn't let up, and soon our entire group of nine was engulfed by a mob that had grown in its fierceness and was beginning to lose any semblance of control. I was frightened and, like the psalmist (Ps. 59:1), prayed that God would deliver me quickly from the hand of my enemies. And like David, the enemies were my own people.

The Diamond District of New York City contains dozens of jewelry stores and is a place of work for thousands of religious Jews, many of them Holocaust survivors. It's not easy to explain to a non-Jew the level of animosity some Jewish people have towards Christianity. Some who attacked us that day blamed the Holocaust on Christians. Many Jewish people do not understand the difference between real Christians and those who merely name the name of Christ, for many nominal Christians have been enemies of the Jewish people.

Jews who believe in Jesus are considered traitors, as though having gone over to the side of the enemy. We are hit, kicked, and yelled at because we are viewed as a threat to Jewish spiritual survival. Every Jew says that if a Jew becomes a Christian, he is no longer a Jew. Jews for Jesus is living proof that this is untrue, but this is one of the reasons Jewish people get so angry with us. If they can make us disappear, then the whole issue of Christ can be dismissed. But as long as we are telling our own people about Jesus and proclaiming the message that one can be Jewish and believe in Jesus, then the gospel in the Jewish community cannot be ignored.

The incident on Forty-seventh Street took place in the summer of 1974, only one of many such attacks during the first Jews for Jesus evangelistic campaign in New York City. Yet since then, we have conducted campaigns there almost every summer. New York is really the capital of the Jewish world, having more Jews there than in all of the nation of Israel. Therefore reaching New York is essential to the vision of the Jews for Jesus ministry.

Our New York evangelistic campaigns aren't like others. It

isn't possible to convince thousands of Jewish people that they should come to Madison Square Garden to hear the gospel preached by a famous person, for Jewish people are gospel avoiders rather than gospel seekers. If the Jewish people are going to be reached, then it will take believers in Jesus going out to them, compelled by the love of Christ and willing to take the risks of confrontation. Jewish people are not going to take the initiative and seek out people who will tell them about Christ.

The reason Jews for Jesus was standing on Forty-seventh Street was our desire to go where our people are and tell them about the Savior. We did not go to antagonize, but to preach Christ, and this was met with an adverse reaction. It was reminiscent of the book of Acts, where Peter's appeal to the Jewish people caused his listeners to be "pierced to the heart" (Acts 2:27). Luke records that thousands accepted Christ that day. But later Stephen, preaching a similar message, encountered a very different response when the Jewish people who heard his message were "cut to the quick" (Acts 7:54) and stoned him to death, making him the first martyr of the church.

A Jews for Jesus witnessing campaign is a rigorous experience. We distribute a few million tracts, usually during the month of July. Back in 1974, we didn't hand out that many because it was our first campaign and this kind of intensive outreach had not been tried before. It's not that distributing gospel tracts is new, but the amount and kind of tracts we distribute are different. The literature is designed to present the eternal message of Y'shua in a contemporary way. Titles such as "Jesus Made Me Kosher," "If Being Born Hasn't Given You Much Satisfaction, Try Being Born Again," and "Shop Till You Drop," capture the minds of New Yorkers.

Campaigners stand on street corners from early morning until late night, enduring heat and humidity, blisters and abuse, in order to make a positive statement about the Lord. Campaigners are argued with, spit at, hit, kicked, but mostly ignored. And sometimes they even get caught in the midst of riots.

Just when I thought that I was going to see Jesus a lot sooner than I had expected, a single overweight, red-faced, very angry New York policeman marched into the midst of the mob. He raised his voice above the crowd and shouted, "Who's responsible for this?"

Quickly, one of the inciters of the riot cried, "They are!" pointing an accusing finger at Baruch Goldstein and me. I was shocked. The policeman shifted his imposing girth towards us and began berating us for causing a riot on "his beat!" The shouts of the crowd began to subside as the policeman took us, the perpetrators, into custody.

In the heat of the moment, Baruch Goldstein shouted, "How can you blame us for the riot? It was them!"

Under his breath the policeman muttered, "Quiet, or I'll never get you out of here!"

It dawned on Baruch and the rest of us what the policeman was doing. It was an unusual demonstration of riot control, but the officer was used to dealing with New Yorkers.

He hollered at the crowd to back off and lined us up two by two. From behind us, he yelled, "Now, each of you, move out!" Slowly, the crowd parted to let us through.

A few kept taunting us as we left, "You're not Jews! You're traitors!" These were echoed by others, "Don't come back! You're Nazis!"

But we kept walking, holding our heads up high, knowing that God had delivered us and that His presence went with us as the pillar of smoke had led the Israelites through the desert.

Can the God of Abraham, Isaac, and Jacob use an Irish New York cop to deliver a group of Jews for Jesus? You bet He can!

As we marched out of the crowd, we sang a traditional Hebrew folk song, "Hineh Ma Tov U'Ma Naim," which means, "Behold how good and pleasant it is for brethren to dwell together in unity." This was our final appeal to the crowd as we marched away under the protective wing of our angelic officer.

Later that day, those of us who had been at Forty-seventh Street gathered with other campaigners at the Jews for Jesus midtown headquarters. This was quite a meeting for me, even more than the incident on Forty-seventh Street, my most memorable experience with God.

The nine of us who were involved with the riot on Forty-seventh Street had gathered to discuss the incident with the twenty-five others who were on the campaign. Moishe Rosen, the director of Jews for Jesus, began the discussion, "If we continue with our witness in New York City, there will be more violence and more of us will get hurt."

Perhaps the incident on Forty-seventh Street happened so quickly that I hadn't had time to consider what it might be like to get beaten and abused for my faith. But now I had time to think, consider, and pray about my worst fears coming true.

Moishe handed out index cards and told us that we could leave the campaign if we wanted and not lose the respect of the group. We took some time and prayed for God's guidance. After praying, I knew exactly what God wanted me to do. I was to stay, to press on, and to make the gospel known to my people.

The author of the book of Hebrews, writing to the early Jewish believers, said, "Therefore Jesus also, that He might sanctify the people through His own blood, suffered outside the gate. Hence, let us go out to Him outside the camp, bearing His reproach" (Heb. 13:12–13). If I was called by the Lord to evangelize the Jewish people, I would often be rejected by those whom I loved and was called to reach. But I was willing to suffer with Jesus outside the camp and take the risks of making the gospel known to my own.

Through this experience I learned something about God, His faithfulness, and the enablement of His Holy Spirit to provide courage in a time of need. Peter and John were threatened by the Temple guards to stop talking about Jesus (Acts 4:21). When they came back to the believers, they prayed. They didn't ask God to deliver them from their difficult situation, but rather they asked for boldness to continue their witness in the face of adversity. God answered their prayer in a magnificent way: "When they had prayed, the place where they had gathered together was shaken, and they were all filled with the Holy Spirit, and began to speak the word of God with boldness" (Acts 4:31). I knew then that God would provide the courage and boldness I needed to stand for Him in a difficult place.

We turned in the index cards and Moishe counted the results. Only one person out of nearly forty asked to leave.

Moishe then announced that we would go back to Forty-seventh Street at the noon hour and hand out tracts again. I was frightened but confident that God would give me the courage to do it.

This time, all forty of us went to Forty-seventh Street. Most of us were dressed in street clothes, but the nine of us who had earlier been in the mob scene in the Diamond District were dressed in Jews for Jesus T-shirts so we could easily be recognized. We had also called the New York Police Department, which sent two plainclothesmen to join us.

Standing on Forty-seventh Street handing out our literature that afternoon, we were threatened, cursed and ignored, but no mobs formed and there were no riots. And we taught ourselves and the people whom we were called to reach a very important lesson: God doesn't give up! He doesn't give up on us and He will not give up on reaching them through us with the good news of Y'shua.

This experience on Forty-seventh Street was so moving for me that I wrote a song at the end of the campaign entitled "The Ballad of Forty-seventh Street." The song sums up so much of what God taught me through this most memorable moment.

Every morning on Forty-seventh Street,
Where the Hasidim come to work,
Cut their diamonds, precious jewels,
Work 'til Messiah comes . . . work 'til Messiah comes.

Jews for Jesus on Forty-seventh Street,
Summer of Nineteen-seventy-four,
Handing out pamphlets, preaching the gospel,
Work for Messiah has come . . . work for Messiah has come.

I'll pour out upon the House of David,
And on the houses of Jerusalem,
The spirit of grace and supplication,
Turn, oh my people, turn . . .

Behold, Messiah comes, Israel,
His scepter in His pierced hand,
Eternal life to Abraham's seed . . .
Turn, oh my people, turn . . . Turn, oh my people, turn.

**Sandra Collareno**

# ~ 2 ~

# How God Speaks to Me

## Sandra Collareno

*Since 1977 Sandra Collareno has been serving the Lord as a missionary in Bolivia, South America, working with the upper-class people, teaching Bible classes, and doing church planting. She was born in Lackawanna, New York, into a Roman Catholic family, making her holy communion and being confirmed at age twelve. All her girlhood days, her ambition was to have a successful business career. She began modeling at age sixteen, and at eighteen began her career in dancing, eventually owning and operating her own dance studios. Several years later, she became a division manager for a cosmetics firm and then, at age thirty-nine, she accepted the Lord Jesus Christ as her personal Savior. She prepared for missionary service at Northeastern Bible College where she graduated in 1976 and in 1987 was named Alumna of the Year.*

---

I was born in western New York state and raised in a Catholic home. My mom died when I was ten years old, and my dad remarried. All my life, I wanted to become a successful career person. When I reached that goal, my life became a series of one exciting venture after another. I modeled for a while, then went into the dance business. Then I left dancing and went to Pittsburgh, Pennsylvania, where I took a job as a waitress in an exclusive restaurant. One night the manager of the beauty consultant department of Max Factor Cosmetics sat at my table. She took one look at me and offered me a job with the company as a traveling representative. At first I turned down the offer, but she left me her card and asked me to think about it. About a month later I decided to accept. She flew me to Hollywood for training. Later my job was that of a supervisor traveling worldwide, hobnobbing with the well-to-do. I opened accounts and taught women how to use and sell the products.

However, after a series of events, I was on the outside looking in, out of a job and not able to find another. After thirty-one interviews and thirty-one closed doors, I began to search for some answers.

About a year before, I had purchased a Bible but never opened it. In my search for answers, someone told me that if I read the Bible and asked God a question, I would have my answer before I finished reading it. So, I asked Him to show me what my life really looked like through His eyes. I started reading with Genesis and read through Revelation. I didn't understand it all but became excited with the Old Testament, wishing we had a God like that today, one that was close to His people. My God had always been distant. I never knew whether He heard me or not when I called or prayed to Him.

At that time I belonged to a health club where I went for exercise, swimming, and massages. One day while having a massage, I asked the masseuse if she had ever read the Bible. I wanted to understand it better and ask some questions. She was a bit surprised and answered, "I read it every day. I am a Christian." I replied, "So am I. I'm a Catholic."

After seeing my hunger to learn more, she began bringing me books to read about the Bible. I read in one that God had a plan for the life of every person and if you wanted to know what that plan was, you had to turn your life over to Him, inviting Him into your life. Right then and there, I asked the Lord to come into my life and take over.

Not really understanding how important that decision was, I did not mention it to anybody. But I kept on reading the Bible constantly with an unquenchable thirst to know more.

Then a few days later, on the last page of a book I was reading a verse of Scripture seemed to leap right out of the book at me in large, bold print. "And everyone that hath forsaken houses, or brethren, or sisters, or father, or mother, or wife, or children, or lands, for my name's sake, shall receive an hundred-fold and shall inherit everlasting life" (Matt. 19:29).

I was so shocked and frightened that I dropped the book and began to cry. Then I realized it was the answer to the question I had asked the Lord six months earlier. Again, not understanding any of this, I said nothing to anyone about the incident, thinking others would think I was cracking up.

The following weekend, the masseuse invited me to her church, the Christian and Missionary Alliance Church in Pittsburgh. I went reluctantly. At the end of the service, the pastor gave an altar call. After the first call, I began to squirm. We were standing in the back of the church. I was wearing a white mini-suit with high white boots and false eyelashes. Feeling very uncomfortable, I kept saying to myself, "No way am I going forward."

After the second call, I began to cry, still not understanding. At the third call, I apologized to my friend, telling her that the pastor was talking to me and that I had to go forward. I practically flew down the aisle. It was as though the Lord Himself were calling me through the pastor's voice, and I *had* to respond. I told the counselors what had happened when I had read the passage from Matthew a few days earlier and they explained to me all that it had meant.

After that, one miracle after another took place in my life. For instance, I was down to my last ten dollars, my rent was due, and my refrigerator was almost empty when I went home for a visit. Well-meaning relatives told me that I had done nothing really different from making my first holy communion and being confirmed. However, when I tried to do the things I had done before that memorable encounter with the Lord, frequenting the places of my former usual activities, something stirred within me and I felt uncomfortable.

When I returned to Pittsburgh, I was confused and prayed to

the Lord for guidance. I visited a priest and explained to him everything that had happened. He told me he had no idea what I was talking about. That night the masseuse, Jean Burke, invited me to a church dinner. After dinner an understanding lady talked to me. She said just to trust the Lord and prove Him. I thought she too did not really understand what I was going through, being single with no one to support me.

That evening when I returned home, I got down on my knees and told the Lord I would go "all the way" with Him until I found out for myself whether or not He was what people said He was. I had been reading a book by A. W. Tozer in which he said that some Christians always leave a back door open just in case what they ask of the Lord does not come to pass. I told the Lord I had no back door. I would go out on a limb and then saw it off by trusting *only* in Him for everything. From that moment until now, He has never failed me. He is everything to me.

The next day, things began to happen. I received two checks in the mailbox the day the rent was due and fifty dollars from the church. The money continued to come in, from where I don't know, but all my bills were paid.

Then I began to think about really studying God's Word. I asked a friend of mine, who was the mother of the registrar at Northeastern Bible College, what it would cost to go there. The college sent me a brochure, but I never paid much attention to it because I had no money. About ten months later, at a missionary conference, the Lord spoke to me through His Word that He wanted me to go to Bible school and then into missionary service. I told the Lord that I would go wherever He led me, but He would really have to lead because I had no idea where to begin.

The very next day a call came from Northeastern asking if I were still thinking about Bible college. I couldn't believe my ears. How God puts everything together! His timing is perfect.

One problem before leaving for school was an outstanding dental bill of two thousand dollars. I knew I must clear that up. After praying, I thought I might offer the dentist my sable stole for his wife as payment for the bill. I explained to him everything that had happened. He said he did not understand and would not take the stole, but so far as the bill was concerned, I owed him nothing. There have been many other miraculous experiences like this as I began to learn more about the faithfulness of my Lord.

I had the opportunity to work my way through Northeastern Bible College. It was there that the Lord began to speak to me about missionary service in South America. The college had a program of sending two students each year to a foreign country as summer missionaries, and I had the privilege of being one of them. We went to Bolivia. It was there that the Lord began to speak to me about a ministry with the upper-class people. Bolivia would have been the last place in the world that I would have chosen myself, but I had promised the Lord I would serve Him anywhere He wanted me to go. I marvel at God's ways. They are so perfect.

Since 1977 I have been in Bolivia, currently serving the Lord in Cochabamba, holding Bible classes and working among upper-class people. We have started a church for them. This was an outgrowth of many classes for couples, children, teenagers, and women. Over the past several years more than seven hundred people have come to know Jesus Christ as their Lord and Savior.

For me, serving the Lord as a missionary has been one of the greatest joys of my life. My only regret is that I did not know Him sooner so that I could serve Him longer. My one desire has been, as the apostle Paul wrote in Philippians 3:10, "that I may know Him . . . ."

As I look back over my life, I can see God's protecting hand upon me all along, opening and closing doors that led to the day when I came to know Him personally. Since then He has led me; supplied my every need, often in miraculous ways; and has given me rich rewards in my work for Him.

**Bruce H. Wilkinson**

# ~ 3 ~

# An Unbelievable Prayer Request

## Bruce H. Wilkinson

*Bruce H. Wilkinson is the president and founder of Walk Thru the Bible Ministries headquartered in Atlanta, Georgia. WTB is a worldwide educational institution whose primary goal is to teach the Word of God in order to help believers mature in Christ. More than one thousand Walk Thru the Old and New Testament seminars are given by over one hundred and twenty-five qualified instructors each year in churches and schools across America, as well as in more than a dozen countries around the world.*

*In addition, over sixty million copies of Walk Thru's four monthly devotional guides have been published. Bruce serves as executive editor for* The Daily Walk, *which leads the reader through the entire Bible in one year;* Family Walk, *which offers daily Bible-based family discussions on crucial topics;* Closer Walk *which covers the New Testament in one year with daily nuggets of truth by great Christian leaders of the past; and* Youthwalk, *which offers daily devotionals for teenagers.*

*Wilkinson has also coauthored* Talk Thru the Old Testament, Talk Thru the New Testament, *and* Talk Thru Bible Personalities. *He was the executive editor of the Bible book introductions and outlines for* The Open Bible Expanded Edition *and served on the Overview Committee for the New King James Version of the Bible. He also served as executive editor for the best-seller,* The Daily Walk Bible.

27

*A board member for a number of Christian organizations in-
cluding the Fellowship of Companies for Christ, Congress on the
Bible, and the Committee on Biblical Exposition, Bruce is listed
in* Who's Who in the World, Who's Who in the South and South-
west, Personalities of America, Men of Achievement, *and* The
International Directory of Distinguished Leadership. *In 1976 he
was named Alumnus of the Year by Northeastern Bible College
and in 1986 he was awarded the Faith and Freedom Award of
the Religious Heritage of America committee.*

*Born in Kearny, New Jersey, on September 4, 1947, into a lov-
ing and committed Christian home, he is a graduate of Northeastern Bible College (B.A., 1969; Th.B., 1970) and Dallas
Theological Seminary in Dallas, Texas (Th.M., 1974). After grad-
uating from Dallas, he accepted a teaching position in the Bible
department of Multnomah School of the Bible in Portland, Oregon, where he served until he resigned in May, 1977, to give his
full efforts to the Walk Thru the Bible outreach.*

*Wilkinson is a speaker in demand across the country and reg-
ularly hosts tours to the Holy Land. He and his wife, Darlene,
were married August 23, 1969. They live with their children,
David, Jennifer, and Jessica in Atlanta where they are active in a
local congregation.*

---

Who would have thought that God would go to such lengths
to prove Himself real to a doubting college student? But He did,
and the impact of that experience dramatically changed the direction of my life.

I had been raised in a godly, committed Christian home. My
parents deeply wanted God's best for my life, and they did all
they could to raise me with Christian principles. Part of that
training included Bible college.

I enrolled at Northeastern Bible College, not because I
wanted to go into the ministry, but solely because my parents
asked me to go for one year as a favor to them. After that one

year, they said I could decide for myself where I wanted to go, but they strongly felt I needed at least one year in a Bible college.

Since I planned to enter the field of engineering like my father, uncle, and grandfather, Bible college seemed to be a waste of time for me. Unfortunately, my resulting poor attitude and semirebellious behavior during my freshman year almost caused my Bible college career to be cut short.

After that turbulent first year, I decided to return to Northeastern only so I could play sports under Coach Walt Wiley. But God had a different agenda for me because, no matter how much I wrestled with them, I couldn't escape the dynamic truths of the Bible taught by professors such as Anderson, Lincoln, Kallam, Johnson, Olsen, and many others. The fact that several faculty members took particular interest in helping me grow up certainly encouraged me to stay there.

During that time of spiritual fluctuation, I kept hearing over and over again in chapel and in the classroom that God is powerful, that He is the Lord of the universe, that He answers prayer, and that the true Christian life involves total commitment. Were those statements really true? I had believed them intellectually since childhood, but I struggled with them internally. If they were true, why did God seem so distant to me? Why did it seem as though He never answered my prayers?

Day after day I'd go through classes and chapel services where the Word was taught faithfully. Frustration grew as I compared my own life to the standards of the Word. I would hear all these truths and yet God didn't seem to be real to me. At least I did not see much evidence of His power in my own life.

By my third year of Bible college, I knew that a showdown was imminent. It was time to find out for certain whether Christianity was really worth giving my life to. So, in an attempt to discover the reality of God, a fellow classmate and I decided to put God to a test. Looking back now, I'm embarrassed by what happened; but I rejoice that God used it so dramatically in my life.

I told my friend, "I'm going to give God one more chance

before I quit it all. I don't want to be a part of Christianity if I have to keep doing it in a half-hearted way. It's either all or nothing. I certainly don't want to be a hypocrite all my life!"

But what could we do to give God an opportunity to show Himself powerful in our lives? How could we personally determine if the God we studied about still parts the Red Sea today?

The two of us decided to construct a prayer request so outlandish that only God could make it happen. If He did answer it, that would be the thing we could always look back on as a certain reminder that God is truly real, alive, and powerful. We decided that if He answered our prayer, then we would give our lives to Him; but if He didn't, then we would drop of of Northeastern and start living life "our way."

We decided to ask God to make someone come along—out of the blue—and ask us to show Moody Science Films in the city of Newark, New Jersey, during the forthcoming summer. We'd never shown even one evangelistic film like those before and had hardly spent any time in Newark, so it seemed so farfetched that it would be the perfect test for us.

We began praying regularly, just the two of us, even in the midst of our rebellious attitude. We told no one. Together we prayed, "God, if You are real, if You are powerful, then we need You to prove Yourself to us. Before the semester ends, have someone come up to us—without our saying anything to anyone—and ask us to show Moody Science Films in Newark."

Weeks went by before God made His first move. Most Bible college students are required to conduct Christian service assignments, whether it's handing out tracts or sharing their testimony somewhere, and this was true at Northeastern. One week my friend and I were assigned to go to the Goodwill Mission in Newark. He was to give his testimony and I was to preach. Frankly, we were in no condition spiritually to minister; but we went with anxious anticipation, wondering if God would do anything about our prayer, since the summer was quickly approaching.

When the service was over, we just wanted to get out of there as quickly as we could. However, a distinguished looking man with graying hair introduced himself as the executive director of the Newark Evangelistic Committee. There was an explosive moment of silence as we wondered what God would do, but we gave no clue to the man.

"You know," the man said, "we're hoping to conduct some creative ministries in Newark this summer, and I was wondering if you two men would be interested in helping us."

I remember my heart beating so fast I thought I would explode! "I don't think so," I stammered. After all, *I* wasn't about to open a door we had asked *God* to open.

But he continued. "I understand you two are students at Northeastern. I'm scheduled to speak there in a few weeks, and I'm meeting with my board of directors before then to go over some new ideas I've got, so why don't we talk after chapel when I'm on campus?"

We agreed to meet with him. As soon as my friend and I returned to my old black Volkswagen convertible, we shouted with excitement. Could God really be answering our prayer? We decided our prayer needed to be more specific—just to make absolutely sure! (Does this sound a little like Gideon's fleece?)

At that time I had just heard about the Open Air Campaigners in Chicago, who had vans specially equipped with generators enabling a movie projector to operate while the engine was running and project onto a screen on the top of the van, or even on the side of a building. On the way back to Northeastern, my friend and I decided that if God was real and powerful, then not only would somebody ask us to show Moody Science Films in Newark, but they would give us a van with the special generator on it!

We returned to our "prayer closet" and began to pray more specifically. We could hardly wait for the day this gentleman came to speak at chapel. What would God do?

Afterwards we met and he took us to a diner in Caldwell for lunch. He was obviously excited about something.

"You'll never guess what happened at our board meeting," he began as we started eating lunch. "A couple of men were in Chicago recently, and they saw something there that we felt will really make an impact on our evangelistic efforts in Newark."

We just nodded. We couldn't believe it! Was God really going to come through?

He continued, "So we voted unanimously to buy a Dodge van. One of our board members is a mechanic, and right now he is adding a special generator to it. What we'd like you two men to do is to show some kind of evangelistic films, something like Moody Science Films, this summer in Newark. Can you do it?"

I almost think you could go into that diner today and find two dents in the ceiling, right over where the two of us had been sitting!

That dramatic diner experience was a turning point in our lives. Yes, our prayer had put God to the test, and by His mercy He had answered magnificently.

Then, true to His character, God proceeded to go beyond what we had asked. He demonstrated Himself so strong and so personally involved in our lives that by the time the summer ended, two different young men emerged.

We didn't know exactly what we were supposed to do, so on the first day of work we went to the director's office in the Newark Evangelistic Committee headquarters. "Well, here we are. What are we supposed to do?"

The director smiled, reached into his pocket, and answered simply, "Here are the keys; there are the films. Now, get creative and win Newark for Christ."

"Win Newark? How? What do we do?"

He winked and replied, "Trust the Lord and develop a strategic plan!"

We walked downstairs, got into the beautiful new blue and white van, and drove around. The two of us began to pray, "Lord, what do You want us to do this summer with these movies?" We soon decided that we wanted to show the movies to as many people as possible.

After riding all around Newark, it soon dawned on us that there were a number of major corporations in Newark. Many had large cafeterias and often would show educational movies at lunch time. So we decided to find the largest ones we could and ask for permission to show our films. Off we went to General Electric, Prudential, and a host of others.

We drove in our van to the headquarters of one Fortune 500 company, approached the receptionist, and said, "We'd like to talk to the president."

"Do you have an appointment?"

"No."

"Whom do you represent?"

I felt like saying "God," but I didn't. "We're here on our own."

"On your own?" she repeated. "To see the president? Without an appointment?"

"That's right."

"What is the nature of your business?"

"We want permission to show religious films to your people at lunch."

She began laughing. But then she called somebody on the phone, and in a few moments the elevator door opened and a man with a dark pinstriped suit and white hair stepped out, walked to the receptionist, and winked.

"Gentlemen," he said, "what can I do for you?" We had no idea who he was, but we explained our purpose.

"Come on upstairs, I'd like you to meet some people," he said. We got in the elevator and he pushed the top button, marked "Executive Offices." When the doors opened, we stepped out on plush red carpeting and walked down a sumptuously appointed hallway toward the only door on the floor. He opened the door and we walked right into an executive meeting!

Here we were, two skinny college students with khaki pants, thin black ties, and white short-sleeved shirts. All the executives wore three-piece suits. We quickly discovered our escort was none other than the president of this national firm!

The president introduced us and said to his board, "Gentlemen, in a summer in which everybody is trying to rip Newark apart and burn it down, I thought it would be healthy for you to see two young men who are trying to rebuild it. Fellows, tell your story!"

So we did. The president said, "Do you have one of these films here?"

"Yes, we have *City of the Bees* down in our van."

"Go get it. Let's see it."

"Right now?"

"Right now." We ran down to the van, brought the film back up, and all of us watched it in their special projection room. The president said, "Are all your films as good as this one?" And God knocked down the walls of Jericho for us at that corporation!

Before long we were showing Moody Science Films every week to the employees of numerous national corporations. God just kept on opening the doors! As a result, thousands of business men and women heard the claims of Jesus Christ on their lives.

All summer long it seemed as though God was trying to over-answer our prayer. We decided the next most strategic use of the films was to show them in large apartment complexes, because there were thousands of kids who had nothing to do at night.

We went to one of the largest complexes and got lost because it was so huge. Eventually we found the man who directed the recreational department and asked him if we could show religious films in the gyms at night.

He answered, "Absolutely not. No religious films can be shown in a government housing project." That was that.

We got back in the van and started to drive away. My partner said, "I know who can get us in there."

"Who?"

"The mayor. Let's go see the mayor."

"The mayor? Do you know the mayor? You've got to be kidding!"

He didn't know the mayor, but we drove to city hall anyway. We got past two secretaries, and the third secretary said, "The mayor has just gotten out of a meeting and has about five minutes before his next one. Can you talk to him in that amount of time?"

"Sure!" So we walked into his palatial office and sat down in front of the mayor's huge desk. We told him our story and asked if he could help us get into these large apartment complexes.

"Sure!" he said, and buzzed his secretary. Then he dictated a short letter that was typed on his personal gold-sealed letter-head: "I hereby highly recommend and support these two men and their purposes for the good of the City of Newark. On the basis of my authority as mayor, please do anything they ask. If you have any questions, contact me personally."

We walked out of that office three feet off the ground! It was just like Nehemiah's letter from King Artaxerxes of Persia to the governors west of the Euphrates River. It opened even more doors for us!

We took the letter to the man in charge of all the housing projects in the entire city of Newark. The result was that we were able to show the evangelistic films to hundreds of children and teens in countless recreation halls during that turbulent summer in Newark.

God's power totally transformed two young men. That summer our faith in Him took root and blossomed because we saw firsthand that He is a God who answers prayer—even beyond what is prayed.

It has been more than twenty years since I first stepped on the campus of Northeastern Bible College as an uncommitted Christian student. As I think back through those eventful years, and especially that dramatic summer, my heart leaps with joy. That incident is one of perhaps half a dozen that have marked my life.

In those college years, not only did God miraculously answer our prayer of testing, but He worked diligently and faithfully through my teachers and coaches, who cared enough about me to put up with me and love me into His will. I know that without their dedication, Walk Thru the Bible Ministries would not exist today.

Thank you, Northeastern! And thank *You*, Lord!

**Esper Ajaj**

# ~ 4 ~

# From Deirattieh, Syria, to Washington, D.C.

## *Esper Ajaj*

*Esper Ajaj was born in Deirattieh, Syria, of Greek Orthodox parents. During his boyhood he suffered discrimination because he was not Muslim. Through Christian relatives in the United States, he came to Northeastern Bible College where he graduated in 1958 and went on to study for a year at the University of Wisconsin. Later he earned a B.A. degree in Christian Education at the Washington Bible College. He was named Northeastern's Alumnus of the Year in 1982.*

*In 1959, he married Jean Leivonen of Newark, New Jersey, whom he had met at Northeastern. They have two daughters and a son. The eldest, Lila, also attended Northeastern and met her husband, Jeff Ross, there. Their son, Philip, and the youngest daughter, Lisa, plan to go to Northeastern, also.*

*Mr. Ajaj had intended to return to Syria as a missionary, but God showed him that his mission field was the Arabic peoples of Washington, D.C. Pastor Ajaj and his wife were accepted by the Evangelical Baptist Mission Board to be their first missionaries to the Arabic-speaking peoples of the United States. As this chapter relates, they have established the Arabic Baptist Church of Washington, D.C., with a congregation of 250 people, and a literature, cassette, and Bible conference ministry all over the country.*

---

In the Middle East if a person is born into a Christian home, he is considered a Christian. It does not matter if he is saved or unsaved, he is counted a Christian by birth. That was my experience. I was born in the town of Deirattieh, in Syria, of Greek Orthodox parents.

My father sent me to a private school until the fifth grade, but after that I attended public Muslim school. By that time we were living in Hamath, an ancient city mentioned in the Old Testament. I was the only Christian in my class and often suffered discrimination because I was not Muslim.

When I was seventeen years of age, I was invited to an evangelistic meeting at the Danish Presbyterian Church. An Egyptian evangelist was holding a series of meetings there and would give free bus rides to and from the meetings, a real treat for most of the youth.

I attended those meetings and one night the evangelist spoke on Isaiah 53. As he went through this chapter, he personalized it by saying, "Christ died for the sins of Peter" and "He was bruised for the iniquity of Mary." I almost heard him say, "The Lord hath laid on Him the iniquity of Esper."

When the evangelist gave the invitation at the end of the service, I went forward to accept Jesus Christ as Lord and Savior, not really knowing the meaning of what I was doing. The counselor at the altar asked me if I were saved. Since I didn't know, he explained from the Scriptures how we can know if we are saved, and I really accepted the Lord that night.

I developed a strong desire to study the Bible, particularly the Old Testament prophecies and their fulfillment in the New Testament. However, Bible colleges or any facilities for formal training were not available in my country. We had relatives in the United States who were born-again Christians, and through them I heard of Northeastern Bible Institute, then three years old. They helped me to apply there after I graduated from high school.

In March, 1954, I arrived in the United States on a Friday, attended church on Sunday, and began school on Monday. Since I could speak very little English, most of my time the first semester was spent in studying the language, with wonderful help from other students as well as the faculty.

Once settled at the college, my big concern was to find a job. One day I went into a grocery store to see if they needed help. But since I did not know the English words for the different kinds of fruits and vegetables, the grocer said he would not hire me. I left very depressed.

I said to the Lord, "God, you brought me here. You know I need to pay tuition. You must provide a job."

Soon after that, as I walked along the road toward the school, I saw two men fixing the tire on their car. I stopped and asked them if they knew where I might find a job. One of the men pointed to a nearby building and said, "Why don't you try there? It is a factory."

When I knocked on the door of the factory, a large German woman opened the door and said to me, "Vat do you vant?" I asked if there was work for me. She said, "Come in! Come in!" It was a toy balloon factory and she showed me all around. I began working there and soon the boss offered jobs to several other Northeastern students. God not only provided for mc, Esper, in my time of need, but He also used this new immigrant to get work for others.

When I began at Northeastern, the school was only three years old and had less than twenty-five students. When I graduated, it had nearly ten times as many. My time there was a period of tremendous spiritual growth for me and exceptional fellowship as I learned about the Bible and the Christian way of life. I also met a young New Jersey woman who was a student. We were married after I graduated and had a year of further study at the University of Wisconsin.

We then went to live in Washington so that I could study more at Washington Bible College. There we met other Christian Arabs. We started having evening meetings together in various homes and gradually formed a church of which I became pastor.

My wife and I had thought of going to Syria as missionaries, but God made it clear that our field was to be the United States. We applied to the Evangelical Baptist Mission Board and were appointed its first missionaries to the Arabic-speaking people in this country.

The general director of the mission told me that he had been praying for fifteen years that someone would work among the Arabic-speaking peoples in the United States. Although he knew what we were beginning to do in Washington, he did not approach me as he wanted the Lord to lead us. And He did.

As soon as the mission accepted us, my wife and I started deputation. We traveled all over the country speaking in churches and raising support for an organized ministry to the Arabic peoples of Washington.

Washington, D.C., is very much like Jerusalem in Acts 2 when there were "Jews from every nation under Heaven." There are fifteen Arabic embassies in the Washington area and people from all of the Middle Eastern countries pass through the city.

Our Arabic meetings in Washington began in the basement of a home in northwest Washington. The congregation consisted of about eighteen adults and children. One day in 1967, a neighbor complained to city officials that a church was meeting in a residence and "that was against fire regulations."

When the zoning inspector came to check on us, he found the chairs and the pulpit that we used, evidence that we had a church meeting there. We were forced to stop.

The congregation had to find other accommodations, but

there was only $400 in the church treasury. We felt the Lord's leading to collect pledges and offerings so that we could look for a building. In one week, we had $1,200. We could start our search.

One day, as we were praying for funds and a suitable building, we heard a bulldozer next door. I went to investigate and found that a speculator was going to build a residence there. We asked whether he would build a church instead. That was no problem for him as long as he got his money.

The cost would be $75,000, staggering for a congregation of eighteen people. The builder demanded $7,000 to begin construction, $7,000 upon completion, and the rest on loan.

I wondered how God could do it. The church began to pray for the additional $5,000 needed to begin construction. A Christian man in his seventies said he would give $5,000 if we would pay him 6 percent interest for as long as he lived. This was the miracle we had prayed for. He gave the money and three weeks later he died. Our church's debt on the first half of our down payment was cleared. Now we had to pray for the second $7,000 we would owe when the church was built.

One of our congregation was a government scientist on sabbatical leave. He had accepted a position with a Massachusetts firm, working a year in the Middle East. That gave him two salaries. He decided to give the church one of his pay checks, $10,000.

It was amazing what the Lord had done for us! The congregation, all in six months time, had received the vision of the building, paid the down payment, and built the building. We now had a sanctuary that would seat 110 people comfortably, and had Sunday school rooms and an apartment on the lower level for the pastor and his family. Many visiting dignitaries from the Arabic embassies and many believers from nearby churches were at the dedication at which we sang "It Took a Miracle."

Since then the Arabic Baptist Church has grown so that more than two hundred and fifty people attend its three services on

Sunday. The sanctuary and Sunday school rooms have been expanded to accommodate this growth. Recently, an English service was begun for the church's younger generation whose mother tongue is English.

Since 1968, the Arabic Baptist Church has had an Arabic literature ministry. It produces a small magazine, *Al Mashal,* which contains Bible studies, testimonies, messages, and news. The magazine has a circulation to more than twelve hundred people in the United States, Canada, and overseas.

Arabic cassettes are also available through the church. Upon request, these tapes that contain messages and/or Arabic songs are sent across North America and abroad.

Not only do Arab Christians across the United States and Canada benefit from the literature and tape ministry of the church, but the annual Arabic Bible Conference begun in 1970 has ministered to thousands of Arabic-speaking people.

The conference is held every Memorial Day weekend at a campground or college campus near the Washington, D.C., area. Up to six hundred people come from all over the United States for fellowship and instruction in their native tongue. In 1986, the first Arabic college/career conference was held in Ohio with fifty-four people from the eastern United States attending.

In addition, I recently published a book in Arabic on soul winning, compiled from a two-month seminar we give on the subject. I also prepared a series of handouts confronting the Islamic religion. These are passed out to Muslims. The book, the handouts, and various articles are all available through the church.

Despite this tremendous growth and outreach of the Arabic Baptist Church, we want to see the ministry expand even more in order to get the Word of God out to the rapidly growing Muslim population. I also have a particular burden to educate Americans more about the Islamic faith to enable them to speak to Muslims more effectively and to protect them from the proselytizing efforts of Islamic propagandists.

I believe Arabic radio broadcasts would be particularly effective, but this is a very expensive undertaking. The Arabic literature ministry should also be expanded. Most importantly, we pray for more laborers to be raised up. The harvest is ready, particularly on the college campuses of the United States. Muslims are growing rapidly in numbers and in strength. We are asking God to raise up others with this same burden who will go forth preaching the gospel and winning souls for Christ. There is a great Muslim mission field in America.

**Barbara Thompson**    **H. Lee Thompson**

# ~ 5 ~

# God Is in Control

## Barbara Thompson

*Lee and Barbara Thompson are veteran church-planting missionaries in Brazil now serving with the Association of Baptists for World Evangelism. Lee was born in Pleasantville, in southern New Jersey in 1941. His was a Christian home and he made a decision for Christ when he was eight years old. Barbara was born in Paterson, New Jersey, in 1942. Hers was a non-Christian home, but she became associated with the young people of the Brookdale Baptist Church of Bloomfield, New Jersey, and accepted Christ at Word of Life Island at Schroon Lake, New York, in the summer of 1957.*

*Both entered what was then Northeastern Bible Institute, committed to prepare for missionary service with a burden for South America. They met there, received their three-year Bible school diplomas in 1963, and were married the day after graduation.*

*The next year was spent in assistant pastor–youth work in Lee's home church, doing deputation to raise their missionary support, and having their first baby, Bonnie Sue. Later in Brazil, their family grew with Philip Harold, born in 1966; Pauline Mae, born in 1969; and Cynthia Beth, born in 1973.*

*The Thompsons' first year in Brazil was devoted to language study in the northeastern coastal city of Fortaleza, and in 1966 they moved to the Amazon Valley. For the next twelve years, they were involved in a church planting ministry in the interior re-*

45

*gions of that vast jungle area. Lee served as field director for ten of these years, and Barbara helped much of this time as field secretary or as field treasurer. Their ministry included the establishment of three churches, discipleship of national leaders, camping ministry, river evangelism, and more. Lee also served for one year as the director of the Christian Home Bookstore in Manaus.*

*The Thompsons were named the Alumni of the Year by Northeastern Bible College in 1979. They were cited for their missionary service in the Amazon Valley of Brazil in pioneer work, boat ministries, church planting, and field leadership.*

*During their years in the jungle, the Thompsons had been hearing about the needs of the urban areas of Brazil where there were fewer missionaries and great spiritual needs. Therefore, in 1979, under the Association of Baptists for World Evangelism they moved to Belo Horizonte, Brazil's third largest city with three million people, in southern Brazil some four hundred miles from São Paulo. In the past seven years, they have guided the first ABWE church to complete autonomy and founded the First Baptist Church of the Cristina housing development.*

*During furloughs in the United States, Lee completed his fourth year of work at Northeastern Bible College and received his Master of Ministry degree from the Baptist Bible Seminary of Clarks Summit, Pennsylvania, in June, 1988. The Thompsons are currently again doing church planting in Belo Horizonte.*

---

Twenty-two years of missionary life and service in Brazil have strengthened our conviction that God, in His sovereignty, has a plan for each one of us and that He is in control of every circumstance of our lives. Lee and I both were burdened to serve the Lord in South America before we even met at Northeastern Bible College in the fall of 1960. The classes taught by godly men there, as well as our Christian service assignments, challenged us further to commit our lives to the Lord for foreign service.

Accepted as missionary appointees with the Evangelical Union of South America (later to be merged with Gospel Missionary Union), we were excited about going to Brazil, yet sad about leaving our families and friends behind. After our farewell church service, one dear lady came to us with tears in her eyes saying, "How could you take that precious little baby of yours down there?" Bonnie was ten months old and had won the hearts of many in the congregation. However, God had called us and we knew He would take care of our baby, too.

We arrived in Belém, Brazil, as scheduled; but the telegram to a missionary there advising of our arrival time had not. Consequently, no one met us in the airport. It was already dark, and we were taken by taxi to a hotel with no idea of where we were. As neither of us knew any Portuguese, we could understand only that we would be staying overnight to catch another plane in the morning. Our tiredness and fears were catching up with us as we realized how helpless we had suddenly become. We barely slept that night.

When morning finally came, we did not know how to ask for breakfast, so we just made do with what we had. We thought we had understood the taxi driver's series of gestures the night before to mean that he would return to take us to the airport by 9 o'clock. The time came and went, however, and we never saw him. A girl at the desk who spoke a little English was able to get in touch with the missionary who hadn't received our telegram and he hurried to bail us out and rush us to our plane. Feeling that the worst was over, we flew to Fortaleza where our own missionaries would meet us and we would begin language studies.

Once again, no one met us, as that telegram had also failed to arrive. However, the Lord sent along a man who spoke enough broken English to help us place a phone call to the missionaries to advise them that we had arrived.

That night we were ready for a good sleep, but it was not to be. Bonnie was so upset by all of the turmoil that she cried the whole night long. I tried to get some powdered milk for her bottle from the kitchen, only to find the door locked and everyone else sound asleep.

Thus began a year of many frustrating experiences. Cooking "from scratch," with no mixes, no frozen foods, and necessary substitutions of basic ingredients got a little easier with practice. The provision of a young national helper also enabled us to handle our new responsibilities better. Not only did she help with some of the food preparations, but she also babysat during the many hours we had to spend in class.

Three months after we had arrived in Brazil, we experienced one of the biggest disappointments of our missionary career. The six barrels holding all of our belongings—household items, wedding presents, musical instruments, slides of our honeymoon, equipment for the work—arrived in Brazil. However, when the barrels were opened in front of the customs agent, more than one-half of the items we had sent were missing. Our barrels had been ransacked while waiting in a warehouse in Rio for a ship to bring them to Fortaleza.

You can imagine how we felt. But imagine also our reaction when we read in our family devotions the next morning, "The bands of the wicked have robbed me: but I have not forgotten thy law" (Ps. 119:61). This timely verse gave us peace to know that God would bring us through the disappointing time.

That experience was typical of our first months away from home. In spite of repeated hard times when our hearts asked Why? we always had a settled feeling that God was in control and that we were where He wanted us to be.

After our language studies were over in April of 1966, we repacked the barrels to be shipped up the Amazon for our next assignment. Brazil is a large country with many distinct cultural regions. Both the climate and the customs of the people in the Amazon Valley are very different from the northeastern coastal city of Fortaleza. Therefore, there were many new adjustments for us.

The remaining three years of our first term in Brazil were spent in Manicoré, a town beside one of the largest tributaries of the Amazon River. Manicoré is referred to by some as the "skid row" of the Madeira River. Those were hard years for us with almost no fruit to show for our labors. Although based at Mani-coré, we were assigned preaching and church planting activities in the settlements all along the river. Transportation was slow and uncomfortable in old river launches that always seemed to be in need of repair. Lee could not take the family and needed to be away almost half the time.

Our Manicoré living conditions were poor, and we battled with sicknesses such as malaria, hepatitis, and intestinal para-sites. Running water and electricity were not available most of the time. We often asked ourselves why God would call a young, healthy couple away from their family and friends to live in a place like this and not bless their ministry with lots of souls ac-cepting Him and getting baptized and discipled for His work. Although we didn't know the answers, we felt assured that we were where God wanted us to be. Perhaps He was using this time to work off some of the rough edges in our own lives and to prepare us for future ministry. In those years, God spoke to me especially through Exodus 14:14: "The Lord shall fight for you and you shall hold your peace." It became my life verse.

After our furlough, a time of rest and fellowship with our fami-lies and friends, we were assigned to Humaitá, a town further into the interior. The news that we were to go to Humaitá did not excite us because we knew that other missionaries had been through a lot of sickness there and that there was much resis-tance to the gospel, but we accepted the Board's decision as God's leading.

In Humaitá, we would be doing the same sort of work that we had done based in Manicoré: traveling the river. Remembering the old, slow launches and our frequent family separations, we wondered how we could prepare ourselves for a more effective ministry.

While we were still at home, we presented to our churches and friends the need for an inboard–outboard speedboat with a small cabin. Within four months, half of the needed funds had come in! Then, one church started a twelve-week "Float the Boat" campaign. Their goal of $1,000 was divided so that each of the Sunday school classes would be responsible to raise a certain amount. This was a small church, but their enthusiasm and faith were great. Small children went home with little boats on which to tape their pennies for Sunday school the next week. We were asked to come to the church to give a boost to the project. After just four weeks, they surpassed their goal! They celebrated with a church banquet with little boats as center-pieces for each table.

This boat revolutionized our ministry by getting us to where we needed to go faster, with less physical strain, and more eco-nomically. Also, often the whole family went along. The Lord blessed our second term, the four years we spent in Humaitá, with many coming to know Him as Savior and being baptized. The small group meetings in a house grew and a church was built in Humaitá. Two churches further in the interior were also established during these four years.

For our third term, we served in the city of Manaus where Lee could execute his responsibilities as field director more effi-ciently. He was manager of the Christian bookstore in the city and also developed the Timothy Program for training national lay leaders in the interior towns. The men were lent cassette players and Lee would make up monthly tapes with studies for them to use in their ministries. It was successful and rewarding.

For several years, however, we had been burdened for Bra-zil's urban areas where there were fewer missionaries and great spiritual needs. In 1979, therefore, under the Association of Bap-tists for World Evangelism, we moved to Belo Horizonte, a city of three million people in southern Brazil.

Just six weeks after we arrived, the wife of our senior mis-sionary died unexpectedly and he returned to the States. He had been the pastor of the only group of believers ABWE had in this big city. Although we were set on planting an entirely new church, God once again changed our direction. The Igreja Batista da Fé (Faith Baptist) of Belo Horizonte asked Lee if he would come and help them, and he consented. Although we had to adjust our plans for ministry, God used this church to help us make the adaptations in vocabulary, city customs, and unique problems Christians face in the city.

Our goal was to make this church indigenous and independent of missionary leadership and financial support as soon as possible. That took longer than we had expected. Three and a half years later, the nationals were supporting the work financially and taking active part in the leadership responsibilities. They called their first national pastor, and we became involved in another ministry to give them freedom to direct the church as they were led.

Two years before we left Igreja Batista da Fé, God had brought a young couple into our lives through tragic circumstances. Onésio and Sandra were planning to be married in January, 1981, when Onésio was in a serious car accident. His cousin was killed, and Onésio went through a trying year spending much time on his back with painful surgeries and recuperations.

Lee started to have Bible studies in Onésio's grandparents' home, where he was staying, in order to encourage him through these trials. Through these studies, several came to know the Lord including Onésio's grandparents and several of his relatives.

In July of 1982, Lee performed Onésio and Sandra's wedding ceremony in São Paulo. They came to live in Belo Horizonte and set up a small grocery store in an enormous housing development called Cristina. There was no established Christian work of any kind in that area, although we continued to have Bible studies with Onésio and Sandra and some of their family members. We put a down payment on one of the modest houses in the development and, using a pen for chickens on the side, made renovations to create a temporary meeting place. We had applied to buy another piece of property for a church building, but government approval did not come for nearly a year.

Since our regular furlough time was drawing near, we decided to extend our term for an extra year. We felt we should not interrupt the successful work in such a promising area where thousands had no other gospel witness.

By August 29, 1983, our chicken coop house was ready for a Sunday afternoon inauguration service. Lee drove around the area announcing the service over a loudspeaker. One family who heard the announcement had no paper to write on, so they scribbled the address on their living room wall! They had been praying for two years that a fundamental church would be started in their development because they were walking an hour each way to church carrying several small children.

To our delight, the meeting place was packed for the inauguration Sunday service. A busload of people from Igreja Batista da Fé and two other groups of new believers in the city came to help with special music and tract distribution. We had people listening from out in the street. When we returned for our next service on Wednesday, we did not know what to expect because we would not have the added number from Igreja Batista da Fé. We were blessed, however, with about forty people. After that, services rarely went below that number and visitors were coming each week.

Thus began one of the most exciting times in our lives. The original house was used for two Sunday school classes for children and the adults met in the renovated chicken coop. Dan and Diana Richner, two missionaries just out of language school, needed experience in church planting, so Diana taught the children and Dan the young people. After our making just one house payment, the group was contributing enough so that it could pick up this responsibility on its own. Decisions for Christ were being made almost every week, and we borrowed a portable baptistry every few months to baptize these new believers. By the end of nine months, more than thirty had been saved and baptized through this outreach.

We were having real growing pains trying to keep in personal touch and ministering with each new member. Also, we needed someone who could play an instrument to keep our singing on key. God sent the man of the household where they had written the address of the church on the wall. A talented guitarist, he also became a deacon and church moderator.

The church called a young national Bible school graduate as its first pastor in December of 1983. Pastor Jorge and his wife, Regina, worked along with us for several months before we left on furlough.

Meanwhile, a two-story building was roughly finished on the property where a church building had been approved for us in a key location in the housing development. Doubling as sanctuary and Sunday school rooms, it was inaugurated just before we left for furlough in June of 1984. Our co-workers decided they would stay on with the national pastor for a few months while he was adjusting to the church. We were on furlough, therefore, before the church even celebrated its first anniversary. Things really moved quickly, and it was thrilling.

After our return from furlough in 1985, our intentions were to start another new church in the city through Bible studies and visitation. The First Baptist Church in the Cristina housing development, however, was having some struggles, and their first pastor had just left. Since national pastors are difficult to find, we stayed on as interim to help them. Nine months later, the church called a pastor from the northern area of Brazil with seventeen years of experience. Things were going well for the church again, and everyone was excited about the potential for growth in the future. The next eight months, however, under this man's leadership were very disappointing. After a stormy and frustrating time, he returned to his former region, and, once again, we were asked to help the church.

After two negative experiences, we were hesitant and discouraged, but God led us to a very sweet couple who now lead the Cristina First Baptist Church. Pastor Valdir and his wife, Hani, have a real burden for souls and know how to disciple people for the Lord. Thirteen people were baptized recently after the church's fourth anniversary celebration. Lord willing, we will be able to start our next church upon our return in June, 1988.

Working with people and seeing God leading in their lives can be a blessed experience when they respond and frustrating when they resist. How wonderful to know, however, that God is in control.

**William P. Mial**

# ~ 6 ~

# "I Being in the Way . . ."

## William P. Mial

*William P. Mial, currently serving as vice president of International Ministries at Trans World Radio headquarters, was born in Paterson, New Jersey, and grew up in a Christian family. His father was a missionary to the Jews in New York City. Bill accepted Christ as his Savior at age seven during special meetings held by Walter ("Happy Mac") McDonald.*

*He earned a B.S. in radio production from John Brown University and also studied one year at Grace Theological Seminary. Bill graduated from Northeastern Bible College in 1957 with a major in Bible. He was named Northeastern's Alumnus of the Year for 1971.*

*Bill first learned about TWR when he heard Dr. Paul Freed speak at Brookdale Baptist Church in February 1958. He and Joan, his wife, felt an immediate and strong call to what was then "The Voice of Tangier" and they sailed in November of 1958 to Tangier for their first overseas assignment with TWR. Subsequent postings included the south of France, Bonaire, Monte Carlo, Hong Kong, Sri Lanka, and Holland.*

*Bill and Joan Mial have two children, Rick and Sondra, and*

*live in Chatham, New Jersey. Rick attended Northeastern Bible
College one year before transferring to LeTourneau College for
engineering studies. Sondra is married to Brad Swanson, also a
Northeastern Bible College graduate, and they are TWR missionaries in Bonaire, Netherlands Antilles.*

---

The thought of reporting memorable experiences with God is
a challenge. Who am I to imply that my walk with God has been
noteworthy, especially a "memorable encounter."

My philosophy of life is that the closer a person walks with the
Lord, the more in harmony the inner man will be with the outer
walk. In other words, rather than striving for encounters with
God, I am looking more for a daily walk in harmony, internally
and externally.

The effect of the antithesis of this lifestyle was impressed
upon me as a young man when I was confronted by a dear
brother in Christ, Merle Fuller, at Highland Lake Bible Conference. I had been caught in an inappropriate activity, and Mr.
Fuller referred to my musical gift as a trumpet player, comment-
ing, "Your playing is beautiful, but your testimony stinks." Since
that time, I have strived to have my walk be an external expres-
sion of my spiritual pilgrimage with the Lord.

I certainly do not want to imply that a close walk with the
Lord results in a trouble-free life. In fact, Scripture speaks
strongly against such a concept when it declares, "Whom the
Lord loves, He chastens." The facing of unanswerable questions
in the light of God's sovereignty will forever be the ultimate test
in the walk of the true believer in Jesus Christ.

With all this as a backdrop, perhaps I can give a few examples
of how my experiences have been a confirmation of walking in
God's way.

The year was 1976; the place, Calcutta, India. After a two-hour delay, the Indian Airlines jet I was on was finally loaded and bound for Madras. After more than two hours, sensing it was time for the plane to be landing, I noticed that the pilot seemed to accelerate, then back off on the jet engines again and again. The plane was flipping violently. The situation seemed out of control and we were undoubtedly going to crash. Fear gripped the face of the passenger from West Germany seated next to me and I reached for the back of the seat in front of me to brace myself for the point of impact.

Moments later, the plane landed on one set of wheels, violently hurdling sideways down the landing strip as the pilot desperately attempted to get it under control.

We had been caught in a heavy monsoon with extremely high winds and flooding of the runway, which had caused the aquaplaning of the aircraft on the tarmac.

Suddenly I realized that I had just stared death in the face and yet had experienced a deep-seated peace that can only come from knowing for sure that one's life is in the hands of the Lord.

A memorable experience with God? Perhaps not, but certainly a sobering opportunity to evaluate the reality of one's faith and to experience the "peace of God that passeth all understanding."

On a subsequent trip to Asia, I was asked to make contact with a Bishop Tudu of Dumka. Dumka is an extremely remote area and I asked myself how I would ever fulfill that assignment.

My first stop on the eight-week journey was outside of Bombay, India, where I participated in a gathering of six hundred Christian leaders in the All-India Congress on Missions and Evangelism. As one of a half-dozen honored guests, I was accommodated in a guest house a few miles from the conference site. The first evening around the supper table I struck up a conversation with the gentleman seated next to me. After he introduced himself, I inquired about the gentleman seated next to him. My heart leaped with praise to the Lord as he said, "Oh, he's Bishop Tudu from Dumka!" A memorable encounter with God? Perhaps not, but an exciting demonstration of the psalmist's declaration, "The steps of a good man are ordered of the Lord."

I shall never forget the day I heard the words, "You need to be in contact with our man Jerry Rankin who is responsible for our ministry in India." "Where does he live?" I inquired. "In Bangkok, Thailand!" At the time I was seated in Richmond, Virginia, with no plans to be in Thailand.

A few months later, I was traveling with Trans World Radio's India executive director, Emil Jebasingh, between Colombo, Sri Lanka, and Madras, India. It was early Sunday morning as Emil and I, deeply engrossed in conversation, walked to the seat selection counter at the Colombo airport. Without any comment, we were handed two boarding passes with seat assignments. "We had hoped to have a no smoking aisle and center seat," I said. "That's what those are," the girl answered. I couldn't imagine how this was possible, having had no dialogue with her, but I felt that the conversation Emil and I were having was much more important that discussing our seat assignments.

We boarded the bus that carried us from the terminal to the plane. As we bounced along across the apron, I glanced at a name tag on a piece of carry-on luggage belonging to a fellow passenger: Jerry Rankin.

When we boarded the plane, Emil had seat 6B, I had seat 6C, and 6A belonged to Jerry Rankin!

As a result of that meeting, there is on the air today a daily fifteen minute broadcast in the Kannada language from TWR's Sri Lanka station. This is being mightily used of the Lord as a strong witness to an area of India that has been historically unresponsive to the gospel.

Was this a memorable encounter with God? Yes, because my experiences in ministry and in life have taught me time and time again that there is a beautiful correlation between "the walk" and "the work" of the child of God. Years ago, the servant of Abraham who had been assigned to find a wife for his son Isaac expressed this concept when he said, "I being in the way, the Lord led me" (Gen. 24:27).

**Marie L. Olson**

# ~ 7 ~

# Not Handicapped, but Not My Fault

## Marie L. Olson

*Dr. Marie L. Olson is associate general director of Hope Town in Carmel, New York, a resident Christian school serving the handicapped. She was brought into the work by "Uncle Win," Dr. Winfield F. Ruelke, founder and president of Children's Bible Fellowship of which Hope Town and the summer ministries, Camp Joy and Camp Hope, are a part.*

*Dr. Olson was born of dedicated Christian parents who loved and cared for her and her brothers. Remembering her childhood, she wrote, "Much of my childhood was spent in church. I was in just about everything there was in church—Sunday school, young people's group, vacation Bible school, morning and evening services, pageants, etc. By the time I was fifteen I was teaching Sunday school, in the choir, and leading the Junior Christian Endeavor. I had accepted the Lord at about seven years of age and at eleven I dedicated my life to the Lord for full-time missionary service."*

*Marie Olson graduated from the Methodist Hospital School of Nursing in Brooklyn, New York, in 1952 and worked there briefly before taking a job at the Public Health Service Hospital in Staten Island. She got her Bachelor's degree through night study at Wagner College. To prepare specifically for missionary work she went as a full-time student to Northeastern Bible Institute and graduated in 1957. After becoming associated with Hope Town she did further part-time study, receiving a B.S. in*

*Christian Education from Nyack College in 1963, a Master's in Special Education from Hunter College four years later, and a Ph.D. in school administration from Fordham University in 1980.*

*She was named the Alumna of the Year in 1968 by Northeastern Bible College.*

---

Sisters get blamed for many things—especially by their brothers. I think I was the only child, however, to be blamed for something as monumental as the Great Depression. Having been born just five months before the 1929 stock market crash, my brothers told me that, following my birth, the whole world fell apart.

Although we were poor during those years, I never really knew that we were poor, because my family was a Christian family and my parents loved and cared for each one of us. From early childhood, when anyone would ask me what I wanted to be when I grew up, I would always answer, "A nurse."

During my second year of nurse's training I fell in love with a young man who was not a Christian. Having been raised to always tell the truth, I was upset to learn—only through God's grace—that this young man had told me many lies and had numerous problems. He was an alcoholic and had been married before having a child whom he had never mentioned. Just two months before our wedding date the Lord allowed these thing to be revealed to me and I was able to end that relationship. It was a very difficult time for me. I wanted nothing to do with the things of the Lord. My Bible remained closed and I prayed only at times of real emergency. I set aside any further thought of missionary service.

After about two years of living a life of deception before the people of the church and some of my family, I sat in church choir one Sunday morning listening to the pastor. I knew that at the end of the sermon he would give an invitation for young people to give their lives to the Lord in full-time Christian service.

I don't know what the pastor said, but I do know that in my heart and mind a very strong battle was going on. I said, "All right, Lord, I won't be a hypocrite any longer. I won't go forward. I'll let everyone know that Marie Olson is *not* going to be a missionary."

When it came to the time of invitation, I don't know how, but I left the choir loft and went to the front of the church, weeping. That very day I asked the Lord to forgive me for my sins of indifference as well as my sins of commission. A large burden lifted from my shoulders and the peace of God flooded my entire being. That day remains as fresh in my memory as salvation does to many. It was one of my most memorable experiences with God.

After my decision to train for the Lord's service, I asked Him to direct me to a school of His choosing. About a week later I attended a service at a church in Yonkers where I picked up a brochure about Northeastern Bible Institute. After reading through that pamphlet, I was convinced that this was where the Lord would have me. In September, 1954, I entered the freshman class. The three years that I spent there were the most special ones in my life.

When I went to Northeastern, I had been a nurse for two full years, with some savings, a small amount of retirement funds, my own car, and a fairly good wardrobe. I didn't have any real financial needs.

While at Northeastern, I saw difficult times. I saw young people who occasionally would question why they were at a Bible institute. But, more importantly, I saw the hand of God working in a mighty way in many lives—especially my own. These were truly years of preparation for missionary service.

Although I had rededicated my life to the Lord and to missionary service, the one place I still did not want to go was Africa. Yet, during my time at Northeastern, I met people whose family members were missionaries there. I heard several missionary speakers from Africa. Finally, one day I said, "Lord, if you want me in Africa, I'm willing to serve you there." This, too, was a special time in my Christian life.

The teachers and staff at Northeastern were special folks, special because of their love for the Lord, their love for teaching the Word, their love for young people, and their willingness to share this and many other things with us. We *saw* God at work. I think in my younger life, having had parents who cared for most of my physical and emotional needs, and a church, in addition to my family, that cared for my spiritual needs, that this was the first time that I saw special things happening in my life. I saw many answers to prayer.

In my last year at Northeastern I was asked to become the school nurse. This meant that I could no longer work at the hospital. The summer prior to that final year, I had spent as the nurse at Camp Joy, receiving a very small remuneration for the entire summer. Now, for the first time, I was facing financial needs. My car was getting older and I needed to travel to Staten Island every weekend to lead the young people's group at my home church. Sometimes I didn't have enough money to pay the bridge toll, but I was determined that I would not ask my parents for help. I felt that at twenty-six years of age I should be able to care for myself. For the first time I saw God supply Marie Olson's needs. I went to the mailbox one day and found a letter from someone whom I had met just one time. It contained fifteen dollars, which met a real need that I had at that time. God is so good!

Following graduation from Northeastern I again served as nurse at Camp Joy. However, my heart was strongly drawn to the boys and girls at Camp Hope, a camp for the physically and sometimes mentally disabled. At the end of that summer I still did not know what I was going to do. With my nurse's training and my Bible School education, I knew that I was prepared to serve the Lord, but I did not know where. The Lord spoke to my heart in such a way that I told Him that I was not going to become involved in the things of the world again, but I would wait until He showed me the place where He would have me serve Him.

Four days before camp ended that summer, Uncle Win (Dr.

Winfield F. Ruelke, founder and president of Children's Bible Fellowship, of which Camp Joy and Camp Hope are a part) asked if I would consider a ministry to the children of Camp Hope.

I told him that I was going to be a missionary. He replied, "Marie, our folks on staff *are* missionaries. Our ministry is a faith ministry and all of our folks are considered home missionaries." As I listened to him my thought was *but I'm going to be a* real *missionary. I'm not going to be a make-believe, stay-at-home missionary.* Then he said, "I have prayed about this all summer long. I don't want you to accept unless you feel, in your heart, that this is the Lord's perfect will for you." He asked me to pray about it, and I told him I would, but I left feeling surely this would not be from the Lord.

Within the next couple of days, it seemed that the more I prayed the more I heard the Lord speaking to me, saying, "Yes, I want you to go out in your own back yard and reach these children." My home was on Staten Island and I considered my back yard as the rest of New York City, a rather large back yard. When I had real peace that Camp Hope was God's place of service for me, I told Uncle Win I would come.

On October 1, 1957, I joined Children's Bible Fellowship to work with boys and girls who are physically disabled. I started classes in hospitals and Saturday clubs with disabled children. I began looking for counselors for our camping ministry and preparing programs for the next summer. I also visited all of our campers in their homes.

I'll never forget going to one home and hearing a mother say, while her child sat at the table with us, "How can there be so many of these kids in institutions. I've tried to get rid of mine but they make me keep him." Her boy had cerebral palsy but was able to walk, could go up and down stairs by himself, feed and dress himself, yet his mother wanted him in an institution. I went down to my car and wept, wondering how a mother could feel that way about her own child.

Over the years, however, I have seen many who seemingly care little or nothing for their own children. One very special verse to me says, "When my father and mother forsake me then the Lord will take me up" (Ps. 27:10). I have seen numerous children—some abandoned, including one actually left in a garbage can—who have come to the place of putting their faith and trust in Christ and who now know the reality and peace that only He can give.

I've know children who have entered into His presence. One muscular dystrophy girl who came from a Jewish background and met the Lord at Camp Hope, said at the end of one summer, "If I'm not back at camp next year it will be because I'll be with Jesus." She did return to camp the next summer but very early in July developed a slight cough and a slight temperature elevation. I started driving her to our doctor, but about a mile from camp she said, "My heart." Then her head slumped over and she entered into His presence.

I think if anyone had told me before camp that one of our children would die that summer I would have taken a leave of absence. However, the peace that flooded my own heart that day was something that only Christians can understand. I *knew* that Susan was with Jesus. Today many of our children from Camp Hope and from Hope Town, who knew that blessed hope, are now with Him.

One day at camp I spoke with a young man, Andy, who did not know the Lord. He was in an angry mood. He wanted to return to his home in Massachusetts. I tried to talk with Andy, but he did not want to listen to me. He said, "You don't understand. You're not handicapped." I said to him, "Andy, that's true. I'm not handicapped, but that isn't my fault."

He looked to me and questioned, "Fault?"

"That's right. I didn't have anything at all to say about the way I was born or what may happen to me. I don't have any guarantee that at some point in my life I may not be handicapped. But this I do know, handicapped or not, I'll be the same person and will have the same Lord in my life, giving me the strength to go through what you need to go through, day by day in your life.

I pointed out another young man with muscular dystrophy, who could do little but loved the Lord and shared many personal blessings by telephone with others from Camp Hope. His love for the Lord constantly showed, and he was willing to share it with others. He, too, is with the Lord now. About a week later Andy asked Jesus to become his Savior.

A big change in my life came just after my fiftieth birthday when I became a mother. I don't know that my days at Northeastern prepared me for motherhood but I believe that my years in the ministry at Camp Hope and Hope Town School did. I know that my years at Northeastern have helped me to be able to share the realities of Jesus Christ in such a way that Lisa, my daughter, now sees the Lord working in her own life.

Lisa, originally named Manyata, was born in India with no arms and legs. She was abandoned by her parents but cared for by a Christian doctor who, when she was two months old, transported her thirty hours by bus to the Ramabai Mukti Mission. She was loved, told about Jesus, and cared for in the mission for the next five years.

When we first began to pray about Manyata's coming to this country, she was three-and-a-half years old. The Ramabai Mukti Mission had requested that we take her to Hope Town so that she might receive the rehabilitation help that she required.

In March of 1979 I received a phone call from a gentleman at Immigration. He told me that he did not feel that our mission spent enough money on the medical needs of our children and he did not feel that we could take Manyata into the country unless we had someone who was willing to sponsor her. I told him that I was not being at all facetious but I truly knew that the Lord would be the One who would provide for all of her needs. He said, "That is very commendable, lady, but the United States needs a little more than that to go on."

Then he asked me why I felt that this little girl should come into our country, that there were thousands of children in the world like this, and that the United States could not be responsible for all of them. I told him that I knew that there were many but that this was the child that the Lord had brought to our attention and I knew she could receive help here that was not available to her in India. As I continued to speak with him, I knew that I was not getting very far. I don't know why I said this, but I said, "I'll tell you this, Sir, one way or another this little girl is going to come into our country." He answered that they would have to investigate further and see if anything could be done for her. We ended our conversation at that point.

I then began to pray, asking the Lord what else He would have me do. As I prayed, I heard the Lord speaking to me, very clearly, just the one word, "Adopt."

I thought I must be hearing the Lord incorrectly. I was approaching my fiftieth birthday and had a cousin just six months older than I who was already twice a grandfather. I felt at my age the Lord wouldn't be expecting this of me. The more I prayed, the more that same word kept coming. I told no one about my prayer concern at that time.

At the end of June, 1979, Uncle Win received a letter from India stating that all medical visas from India had been stopped and asking directly, "Would Miss Olson, or someone at Hope Town consider adopting Manyata?"

Now I saw what I had been praying about expressed in writing. At that point I told Uncle Win that I had already been praying for about three months concerning this matter. I asked him if I might speak with a lawyer about it. He said, "Yes, but take it slowly." He wanted me to be very sure what the Lord would have.

I called a friend who lived in Carmel, who had already adopted a boy who was born without arms. She gave me the name of a lawyer in Hicksville, Long Island. I told the lawyer of my concern for Manyata, but that I was still not sure adopting her was the thing to do. I told him that I was now fifty years of age. He said that my age did not matter. I told him that I was single, never having been married. He said that did not matter either. The lawyer then asked me, "Do you love this little girl?" "Yes, I do love her, even though I have never met her and have only seen her picture." He said, "Then I think you ought to adopt her."

I told the lawyer I'd continue to pray about it but that I would like to start the paper work. Months went by without my hearing anything.

I went to Fordham that fall semester but decided not to go to school for the spring semester, since I felt that Manyata would be coming into my life and I would need to spend more time with her. I asked the Lord to make it possible for me to get the word in time for me to have the entire semester with my new little daughter.

The next day an airmail letter arrived from India. I read, "Dear Miss Olson, we are pleased to inform you that you have been granted guardianship of Manyata."

I decided to keep the name Manyata, which means "acceptance," as her beautiful Mahrati middle name and call her Lisa as a first name. Then I made arrangements for a flight to India in two weeks. When I arrived in India about two o'clock in the morning, I worked my way through the many taxi drivers who were literally trying to pull my suitcases out of my hands. Then I heard a voice calling my name. I looked up to see a friend from the mission holding Manyata in her arms. I hurried to them and hugged and kissed my little one for the first time. Naturally, at that time of morning she was extremely tired and just gave me a blank stare.

In the taxi going to the hotel, I held Lisa on my lap but she would not look at me and just stared straight ahead. In the next five days I had a difficult time, for this little girl would not allow me to feed her or get close to her. I felt that she did not even like me.

As I spoke to Dr. Sheela Gupta, the doctor at Mukti, she told me that Manyata was testing me. Naturally, she had no idea where America was nor what kind of a person I was. I must give her time. We continued to pray. We were then allowed to go to Supa, which is an outstation about ten miles away. It was only Nita, an Indian woman, Manyata, and myself. We spoke a great deal of English to Manyata and I was writing, phonetically, Indian words that I felt would be of help to me as I took Lisa back to the States.

From there we went to Bombay and Manyata allowed me to become closer to her. I could feed her and talk to her more openly. She loved my tape recorder, loved to talk into it and hear herself as I would play it back. We also did some singing on the tape so that I would have her little voice in Mahrati.

As we returned to the airport early in the morning, Nita was allowed to go through much of the area with me. However, just before I got on the plane, she told me she was going to leave. She gave me a peck on the cheek and was off.

At that point they were examining the contents of my purse and doing a body search on both Lisa and me. As we went into the waiting room, Lisa realized that Nita (or Moushee, as she called her) was not with us. She started to cry and called over and over, "Moushee, Moushee, Moushee." I took her out of her stroller and onto my lap, while tears were streaming down my face, and kept repeating over and over, "Mommie loves you, Moushee loves you, Jesus loves you." I said it over and over for about ten minutes until she stopped crying and quieted down. The trip home was long but Nita had given her a tranquilizer to help her sleep. About an hour before we were to arrive in New York I told her that we would soon see Uncle Win, whom she knew, and many other people, and that we would be going to our home.

After a loving welcome, including a beautiful corsage for Lisa, we returned to Hope Town and there began the strong bond that has developed between a mother and daughter. Yes, we had a few difficult times but in those next three and one-half weeks there were only about four times when I could not understand what she was telling me nor could she understand what I was trying to say to her. She started nursery school and learned much from the other children.

Lisa came to the point of salvation about one month before her sixth birthday when I had the privilege of introducing her to Jesus Christ. She, too, has seen the Lord do miraculous things in her life.

Lisa now attends public school, drives a car (electric) and an electric wheelchair, writes very well, and has many friends. Her desire is to show others what He has done for her. Her prayers are usually very direct. She knows the One to whom she is speaking. How good it is to know that, despite the handicap that will bring stares and questions all of her life, she has a God who cares, will sustain, guide and help her, and will one day give her a new body like unto His own glorious body.

I rejoice in the privilege that has been mine to share God with others, sometimes in a classroom, sometimes in a dispensary, sometimes at home, sometimes in a church. But, it does not matter where He is shared, it matters only that we share Him.

Though there have been many changes in my life, I'm thankful for the privilege, for the past thirty years, to have served a God who does not change. He is *so* good! He has given me many memorable experiences. "Great is the Lord and most worthy of praise: His greatness no one can fathom" (Ps. 145:3 NIV).

**Robert A. Johnson, Jr.**

# ~ 8 ~

# In North Carolina God Spoke

## *Robert A. Johnson, Jr.*

*Robert A. Johnson, Jr., currently is CBM Ministries, Inc., director for most of North Carolina and some adjoining territory. He was born in Passaic, New Jersey, in 1935 where his father was a bank clerk who felt the call to full-time missionary work at the family's home church, Brookdale Baptist. Under the church's pastor, Dr. Charles W. Anderson, Bob, Jr., accepted Christ as Savior at age eight. When his father became a member of the Children's Bible Mission, the family moved south to North Carolina.*

*In 1957 Bob married Deborah Dugan and entered what was then Northeastern Bible Institute to prepare for a lifetime of service with the Children's Bible Mission. The Johnsons have two sons, Robert Kryn Johnson, born in 1959, and Timothy Cairns Johnson, born in 1962.*

*In 1980 Robert A. Johnson, Jr., was named Alumnus of the Year by the faculty of Northeastern Bible College.*

---

The fall of 1944, when I was eight years old, found our family packing our belongings to leave New Jersey and move to the mountains of East Tennessee to work with the Children's Bible Mission. Under Dr. Charles W. Anderson, at the Brookdale Baptist Church in Bloomfield, New Jersey, my father had felt the call to go into full-time Christian work.

This was a time of learning for our family. Money was scarce and it was very difficult for my Dad to provide three meals a day for a wife and two children. However, during those times, the Lord taught us many valuable lessons. I recall when my Dad's bank balance was down to ten cents and we had no food in the house. Our prayers were answered when we received some cans of clam chowder sent from a friend in Long Island. God knew our need and was right on time.

The winters in northeast Tennessee were cold, and it was my job to keep the wood bin full from the pile in an open basement under the house. With much harsh weather, I could see the wood pile growing smaller and smaller and finally there was nothing more to pick up. This need became a matter of prayer. The next morning we thought that the Lord had provided when we heard the rumble of a big truck backing down our alley, dumping its contents of wood under our house. We were praising the Lord as the truck drove off thanking Him for providing once again. Our smiles were short lived, however, when the truck reappeared in front of the house and the driver came to the door. He told us that he had made a mistake and that wood that he had dumped under our house was to be delivered two doors down the block.

Did God make a mistake? Didn't He know that we needed that wood more than the folks two doors away? The men proceeded to back their truck up to "our" pile of wood and throw it back on. Little did we know that the Lord was still working, for soon the men got tired of picking up all the pieces and left us enough wood to heat the house for two more days. When that wood supply was gone, we found a check in the mailbox to buy some more. God was only giving us a little test and once again He was faithful.

During another winter, I remember that all I had was a thin jacket. My Dad told me that the only way I could get a nice warm coat, would be to sell a U.S. war bond that I had worked hard to get. That was hard for me to do, but we were richer spiritually than materially.

Children's Bible Mission, the organization with which my Dad worked, had a summer camp program for boys and girls. In my early teenage years, I found myself in camp doing what I could to help, such as carrying boxes of food, cleaning, and working in the snack shack. I enjoyed these times but wasn't quite sure that I wanted to be poor for the rest of my life.

The summer between my seventh and eighth grades, our family moved from Tennessee to North Carolina. CBM needed a director to head the work in Raleigh and be in charge of the entire state. With a borrowed truck and a worn-out car, we moved. Our first home was a big old farmhouse where an old preacher lived by himself. He was glad to have us since Mom gave him good, home-cooked meals in exchange for a reduction on the rent.

Not long after that, an acre of land was offered to my Dad. He and I worked together to build our first real home in North Carolina. I was then about fifteen years old and felt lonely way out in the country, with few friends.

When not in school, I worked for a farmer nearby plowing cotton, pulling corn, and doing a variety of other jobs. My long evenings gave me plenty of time to think. I remember one New Year's Eve listening to the New Year coming in on the radio from Times Square in New York.

Although I had been saved about seven years earlier, for some reason I had some serious doubts about my salvation that night. In my bedroom, I told the Lord that I wanted to be sure of my salvation and I settled it then in my own mind. To this day, I have never felt that way again.

At that point in my life, I lived for the day when I would be sixteen years old. I had driven a lot of farm tractors, but I wanted to get behind the wheel of a car. On my sixteenth birthday, I got my driving permit in the morning before school and my driver's license after school. Ten days later, I passed my test to drive a school bus.

During the summers, I continued to be around the CBM camp. After passing the Red Cross life saving test, I became what many guys dream of being, head lifeguard. All of a sudden, I had girls hanging around, talking to me, and wanting to take pictures. I didn't mind this a bit. Camp was fun and I enjoyed it but I wasn't sure I wanted to do it for a living. I continued to see my Dad struggle with the camp's bills and with his own.

After graduation from high school in 1953, I moved to New Jersey to live with my aunt and uncle. I had plans to make more money than my Dad. My first job as a carpenter's helper accomplished that. Six months later, I began to work with the engineering department of a railroad. In this job I made more money than my high school principal earned back in North Carolina. I bought my first car and things were going fine.

I attended our home church, Brookdale Baptist Church, and sat under the ministry of the man who was speaking the night that I was saved, Dr. Charles Anderson. I got involved with the youth group even though I was a bit older than most of the other members. The group visited a rescue mission in New York City one time and gave out tracts in the center of Newark another time. These outings left an impression on my life.

The Lord continued to work in my life and soon I became discontented with my job. Some of the men in the office where I worked advised me to quit my job, return to North Carolina, and get a degree in engineering from North Carolina State University. Before long, I was back home going to college and again working at camp during the summer. I loved engineering but God seemed to lead me in that field for only two years.

During the summer of 1956, a young lady, Debbie Dugan, came to play the piano at camp. We soon found ourselves very attracted to each other and before the summer was over, I asked her to be my wife. Debbie had a real love for children all that summer at camp and through that, I began to see the spiritual needs of boys and girls, and how God could use me to help meet those needs. It seemed like putting on a well-made glove. Debbie and I were meant for each other and together the Lord meant for us to serve Him in children's work.

Things happened very rapidly after that. By Thanksgiving, we were engaged and the next August we were married at the close of the camp session. One month later, I became a student at Northeastern Bible Institute. Debbie had graduated from

Wheaton College, and so she began to teach school while I worked part-time in a truck repair garage. The Lord supplied our needs in many ways during those early days of our marriage.

Northeastern was hard for me. Having grown up in a Christian home and attending Sunday school all my life, I thought I knew a lot. I soon found out how much I didn't know. During my first semester at school, I had the flu and ended up failing my Bible Doctrine final exam. What a way to start! However, I knew that the Lord wanted me there and so I just kept plugging along and managed to stay above C level in grades.

Nevertheless I looked forward to the summers when we would head for New Life Camp in North Carolina where we felt the Lord's call for us.

After two years at Northeastern, we decided to start a family and on December 7, 1959, our first son, Bobby, was born. Debbie stopped working but somehow all the bills got paid. We thanked the Lord for that.

I am thankful for my days at Northeastern. I met some very godly men and women there who had a real impact on my life. I saw people who were not interested in making a lot of money, but were more interested in the real values of life and in training others.

Upon finishing school, we packed all our possessions in an old truck and headed south to get camp ready for another season. I enjoyed going with another worker to schools that he visited each month where children memorized three hundred Bible verses so that they could come to camp free for a week. My friend held a thirty-minute chapel program in the schools, telling a Bible story using visual aids, and encouraging the children to keep on working on their Scripture memorization. That summer between twelve and thirteen hundred boys and girls came to camp and many of them were saved. With three hundred Bible verses already tucked away in their hearts, they were like ripe fruit ready to be picked.

During that summer of 1962, the Lord sent us another son, Timothy. After the summer, I was to be on my own with my own circuit of schools, but I discovered that some of the school authorities in my territory had decided not to have our program anymore. We were disappointed but felt that this was the Lord's way of pushing us farther out to schools in new areas.

Soon, I had twenty-three schools to visit every month. This was exciting work. Many of those school children were saved during their first summer at camp. Since they desired to return for another summer, our office sent them Bible lessons each month. Debbie corrected lessons, which gave her contact with the children.

Even though everything was going well, I continued to have the tug of the foreign field on my heart. At first I put it aside with a strong no. As I tried to put it off, God continued to ask me if I would be willing to go anywhere. Finally one night when I could not sleep, I told the Lord that I would be willing to go anywhere that He would lead. Going back to bed, I had no idea just where that commitment would take me.

The answer finally came nine months later when I was elected to the Board of Directors of our mission. All that time, the Lord planned to keep me right where I was serving Him. He just wanted a willing vessel. God's further confirmation of where He wanted me came in 1976 when I was elected president of our national board. I served in that capacity for the next four years and am still on the board today.

With more and more leadership responsibilities, I soon had to give up my monthly visits to the schools. Other workers came along and took this responsibility, but I missed seeing all those happy faces each month.

During those years in CBM, I had been working under the leadership of my Dad in the North Carolina Division. Upon his death in 1978, I was asked to assume the role of state director. The Lord was good to have given me all those years of experience in preparation for such a position.

Our Raleigh New Life Camp has continued to minister each summer to thousands of young people. Hundreds are saved, their families also are blessed, and many go on into full-time Christian service. Our work has also expanded to make the camp a base for year-round activity with youth groups. We know the Lord has spoken to us in, and for the sake of, North Carolina.

**Alan and Barbara Bachmann**

# ~ 9 ~

# God's Hands on Us

## Alan Bachmann

*Alan Bachmann, for thirty years, with his wife and family, a missionary in various parts of Brazil, is now on loan from the Gospel Missionary Union to Trans World Radio. Since 1982 he has been executive secretary for Radio Trans Mundial do Brasil. He directs Portuguese language broadcasts for South America, Europe, and Africa and travels widely from São Paulo headquarters.*

*Alan was born of a German heritage in Nutley, New Jersey, in 1936. His parents came to know the Lord under the ministry of Dr. Charles W. Anderson at the Brookdale Baptist Church. They soon moved to Massachusetts where Alan grew up. There at a school dance he met Barbara Wheeler who came from a traditional New England family. They both became dedicated Christians and active in student evangelism.*

*In the summer of 1954 Alan worked on fishing boats off the Jersey shore and Barbara at the Harvey Cedars Bible Conference. That gave opportunity for evening meetings together where missionaries often spoke.*

*One missionary who especially impressed them was Phil Saint, a chalk-talk evangelist, who spoke of the unreached tribes of South America. (Two years later his brother Nate was murdered by the Auca Indians of Ecuador.)*

*By the end of summer Alan and Barbara had decided to go to Northeastern Bible Institute to prepare for foreign missionary service. A year and a half later, they were married. Following graduation from Northeastern in 1957, they studied at the Summer Institute of Linguistics at the University of Oklahoma and at the Biola School of Missionary Medicine in Los Angeles.*

*Raising support, they lived and worked in New Jersey and renewed acquaintance with a Northeastern teacher, William Lincoln, who appealed to them to develop a river boat ministry on the Madeira River in the Amazon jungle of Brazil. Alan was ordained, and they were accepted by the Gospel Missionary Union for work there. By that time they had two children, Beth, born in California, and David, born in New Jersey.*

*Their Brazilian experience began in 1960 with a year of Portuguese language study. Then came twelve years of church planting and river boat evangelism along the Madeira River where their medical training was especially helpful. Recognizing their service, the Bachmanns were named Northeastern's Alumni of the Year in 1970.*

*The next period of service was ten years at Manaus, the capital of the state of Amazonas, to lead a literature ministry. This involved showing Moody science films in schools and hospitals, speaking on a daily live radio broadcast, and opening literature centers.*

*The children went to national schools. With her husband, Beth is now a missionary in Amazonas. David and his wife are missionaries in church planting and radio ministries in Manaus. Paul is trained in aviation mechanics and, with his wife, looks forward to missionary aviation work in Brazil. Timothy is in his third year at Word of Life Bible College, preparing for the ministry. Daniel finished high school in São Paulo while working full time as a computer programmer and now is in college in the United States.*

Brazil was presented to us many times in our studies, and we began to meet new friends from that far-off land. Yet, even then, it was not Brazil calling, but God saying, "Go." Soon we were on our way, traveling by ship to Brazil with two small children.

Our first assignment was a thousand miles up the Amazon Valley at the settlement of Manicoré where we began church planting and river evangelism along the Madeira River. From this hub, we began our journey upstream towards Bolivia, with our destination several days beyond the islands and treacherous waterways that lay before us. We came to love these waterways. Our children did too, and they are still there today. We also came to love the people who lived beside the waters and back into the jungles, past the waterfalls and near the lakes, far from the twentieth century.

It was during one of these journeys by river launch, up the raging torrent of water called the Madeira River, that I had a memorable experience. With torrential rains falling and night descending quickly, we tied up in an eddy of current just before the rocks and raging waters that we would face the following morning. As I lay in my hammock, I thought of my wife and children upriver, snug in our home, awaiting my arrival a couple of days hence. The night sky was ripped and slashed by lightning. The crashing thunder competed with the beating rain on the launch roof and the hum of mosquitoes inside.

At dawn, we enjoyed our simple breakfast of bananas and coffee. Then we hand-cranked the diesel engine and chugged out into the main stream between two jutting rock piles, through which the current poured with mighty force. The tiny old engine seemed to plead for help as it fought the surging waters. At the wheel, I strained to guide our river boat safely beyond the threatening obstacles.

Just as it seemed that we had won the struggle against the current and the rocks, with a sudden gasp, the engine quit. The rocks were right behind us. Immediately, I cranked the wheel of the launch fully to the right, but the current took over and swung us against a vertical bluff at which the river was chewing away.

One of the two men with me wrapped the chain of our launch around his shoulders, grabbed his machete, and swiftly climbed the clay embankment, cutting hand holds straight upward, as the other man and I clawed at the embankment to keep the boat from washing out of control into the rocks. In what seemed like hours, but was only moments, we two also were climbing up the side of the bluff while the man above held a long chain to secure the launch. Looking back, we saw a vertical crack in the bluff, a bad sign.

When we reached the top, we struggled against the rain, the slippery mud, and exhaustion, to ease the river launch slowly along the bluff to where the land slanted down to the river and the current eddied behind a point of land.

As soon as we had beached the boat and moved away from the high promontory, we were startled by a sound, like a loudly whispered swish. There, before our eyes, the whole side of the clay embankment, where we had just been, tumbled into the raging current, sending a mighty wave across the river. But for the difference of a few moments, we would have been under the earth, not safely away from it.

Certainly God had a purpose and a lesson for us in what had happened. Exhausted and trembling, we tied up the river boat and, standing there with the muddy Madeira River below us, bowed our heads and thanked the Lord for His grace.

Later I had another unforgettable experience.

The little town of Manicoré, with four thousand inhabitants, was perched high on a bluff, tight in the curve of the mighty Madeira River. A mile wide and raging deep in the rainy season, in the dry season the river was forty feet lower and calm, with huge sandbars to complicate travel for the river boats that traded with the people along the liquid highway.

We had lived at Manicoré for several years. Looking out over the river was our church; and on this Sunday the evening service was over. We had just come home and set our chairs overlooking the river to enjoy the coolest part of Amazon life, a quiet evening breeze off the river. The Aladdin lamp was lit in the front room of our clay and wood house, and the children were snuggled in their hammocks under mosquito nets. Another day was over. Rest, at last.

Just then one of the men from the church came running to us in distress. On his way home, he had heard voices and murmurings in the town square. Shielded by bushes and unseen, he had drawn closer. He overheard men planning to drive the evangelical missionary family from the town, and he feared for our lives. He ran to warn us, pleading for us to leave town and flee by river boat.

We felt that God had brought us here and that He was not directing our departure. We did not go, and nothing happened.

Several years later when we were living a couple of days upriver, I returned to visit Manicoré. I was in one of the stores arranging medicines on the proprietor's shelf. People had a way of buying their medications by the pretty colored boxes, and I wanted to help the store keeper to label the medications by the cause of the illness: leprosy, tuberculosis, leishmaniasis, malaria, parasitic infestations, and other routine illnesses of our region.

While I was working, the boss asked me, "Do you remember the night when we were going to run you out of town?"

Shocked, and trying not to show my reaction, I answered, "No, what happened?"

He told me this story. As the men gathered to go to our home, carrying ax handles, hoe handles, and machetes, in the darkness appeared a man dressed in white, who rebuked them with a powerful voice: "Leave these people alone. They are God's. Do not touch them." The men dropped their weapons and fled.

I asked who had spoken. He said he did not know. Insisting that he knew everyone in town, I asked again. But he insisted that the man was a stranger who spoke with authority. No one had questioned the voice. Could it be other than God who had protected us? It wasn't Brazil that had called, it was God who sent.

We had a third memorable experience when we were living far in the jungle about five days by river from what most people would call civilization. Our son Daniel, just a few months old, had had a bad cold and now was fighting for his life with a raging fever. In the open jungle house, with only partial walls dividing the rooms, I sat with Danny in my arms, rocking him. I felt helpless.

At their weekly meeting in our living room, the native women and Barb were pleading with God. He heard, and I sensed a response in Danny's body. The rolled back eyes, the convulsions, and the burning fever seemed to leave his body within a matter of moments. He relaxed and looked at me. God had done something exceptional just when it looked as though Danny was ready to leave us.

The women did not seem surprised. They had expected God to hear and answer. Was our faith less? Were we too rational to expect the unexpectable?

A different but equally memorable experience occurred when we were living in a town of eight hundred people where a bishop, three priests, and about a dozen nuns ruled with strong hands and sharp eyes, keeping vigilance over "their people."

A building in the village was called a hospital. It contained simple living quarters for the sick and for expectant mothers. Run by some of the nuns, it had no professional medical staff and nobody expected it. We were a long way from the twentieth century in this corner of the jungle.

One day the mother superior sent word asking me to go to the hospital. I went with surprise because never before had a Protestant been seen within the walls or courtyard of the hospital. The little brown fellow from along the river who bore the message from the nun, told me a woman was struggling to deliver her child. The struggle had been going on since the day before. Hoping for the best but expecting the worst, I took what instruments I thought necessary. As I entered the courtyard of the hospital, murmuring was strong, sounding as though no one wanted to let a Protestant into the inner reaches. Nevertheless, I proceeded with no physical resistance.

The woman was on a delivery table in the maternity ward. She was a big girl, but had struggled long and was obviously exhausted. I learned that none of the proper preparation for delivery had been done, complicating the struggle for the mother-to-be.

The woman was eclamptic and had evidently had more than one seizure already, for her tongue and lips were lacerated. Just then she went into another seizure and within moments, it became apparent that she was experiencing cardiac arrest.

With God's help measures were taken to revive the woman's heart beat, respiration returned, and I was able to deliver the baby who had apparently died the day before. It was a sad experience, but it was a miracle that the mother lived. I left the hospital knowing that if both mother and child had died, I could have been assaulted in the courtyard.

God was good to us, and in later years, as the gospel gained ground and a church was built, we could look back and see why He had put us through experiences such as that. The town of eight hundred that received us as the first evangelicals has now grown to about twenty-five thousand, with four evangelical churches.

Finally, let me tell you about God's hands on our family. Our son Tim was nine years old when his grandmother asked him, "Timothy, when you grow up, are you going to be a missionary like your father?" With a very severe frown, he replied, "Grandma, I already am a missionary!"

Barb and I always felt that our family must feel that God cares for each one of us, or mom and dad would have no ministry at all. The children in the Bachmann home had full participation in the work God called the family to do. They went to the local schools where they faced persecution. They carried water from the river for drinking and for washing. They did chores, treking down the muddy road at dawn to the local wood-fire bakery to get bread for that day's breakfast. They helped slaughter a chicken in the backyard and prepare it for eating. They traveled the rivers and jungle trails, each in their turn, with me.

When people came to our home for help, they held the screaming, wriggling babies who needed injections, and they calmed the fears of the children who had to have a tooth pulled. They held the light for emergency surgery, or scrubbed in and helped sew up the incision. It was just what the family did.

Barb, of a jungle evening, climbed under the mosquito net and into the hammock. Each child in his turn heard a story, maybe read in English but with the commentary being in Portuguese. Our children grew up sharing with us a God-given love for an unloved people. We wanted them to see Jesus in us, and then listen to us tell about Him.

And so it was that five little jungle-bunny Bachmann kids grew up sharing life with a mom and dad whose lives were being shared with hundreds of people all over the Amazon region. Today they are still there, with their children, carrying on God's work. Jonas and Beth, our son-in-law and daughter, as Brazilian pastor and wife, run a thriving church in the little town of Manicoré (meaning "spirit of a pig"), where not only is a church thriving but also a Christian Day School.

For years Barb and I had a radio program in the Amazon, now broadcast by David and his wife. Paul, from the earliest, was superobservant when steering the fast-skipping boat between logs and sand bars. He was often one step ahead of me with the right wrench when fixing the engine. Today he flies airplanes and repairs them, too. Soon, in aviation ministry, he'll be poking through the clouds over the rivers he used to run with his dad.

Late one dark night a call came at our door and inside was brought a man slashed to pieces by a jaguar. He was laid on our dining room table while Bethie and Barb began heating water and lighting lamps. We had to sew up over fifty lacerations but the man from the jungle pulled through. There were other times when it was one of our own kids who became the object of our sewing, as when Danny jumped off the sofa of woven vine furniture and fell onto the wide, uneven boards of a hardwood floor.

Other times Beth or one of the boys would follow me to a sick person's home, carrying the instruments, or helping to "catch" the baby. It was all in the family, throughout our life: a lot of fun, a lot of learning, trying whenever we could to say to someone, in God's name, "We love you and want to help."

**David M. Virkler**

# ~ 10 ~

# Heir Waves

## David M. Virkler

*David M. Virkler, a Northeastern Bible College graduate in both diploma (1956) and degree programs (1986) and Alumnus of the Year for 1969, founded Dedication Evangelism in 1961 after completing a five-year pastorate in Montclair, New Jersey, where he was ordained to the ministry. He conducts hundreds of services annually in churches, camps, conferences and retreats, and a variety of specialty ministries including teaching broadcasting courses in colleges and camps. Dave produces "The Word and the World," a quarter-hour weekly broadcast aired over thirty-three outlets, and a daily, one-minute "Newspoint" available to any station. Other ministries include literature and cassette distribution. He has had several articles published in national magazines, and is an officer of the Eastern Chapter of National Religious Broadcasters.*

*Dave is married to Thelma (Axman), Northeastern Class of 1956, who has been vitally involved in his ministry. They have four children and live in Towaco, New Jersey, near the ministry headquarters.*

---

Everyone tensed as the giant sweep hand on the studio wall clock crept toward air time. Informal chatter trailed off into jittery quiet. The red light blinked on, boldly announcing On the Air. The Reverend Clyde Gault, intense young pastor of the Beacon Gospel Tabernacle in my upstate New York hometown, sped through his welcome and quickly introduced the male quartet, which cued themselves into musical gear off mike with a pitch pipe, since no pianist was available. Stepping in close, Hans, Art, Frank, and Paul broke into a rousing gospel song, blended by practice and dogged determination. Paul, who sang in that enthusiastic laymen's foursome, was also my father.

Gault preached with rapid-fire delivery, urging his unseen audience to heed the claims of Christ, generously lacing his fervent message with Scripture. Gault's jacket slowly dampened as perspiration soaked his best and only Sunday suit. The quartet cued themselves again, edged in for a final song, and stepped back from the mike, fading down while a closing announcement wrapped things up.

Quickly it was over. The red light winked off, Gault relaxed, and everyone breathed easier. It wasn't very professional, but it was obviously sincere. Farewells were said and we left for our various Sunday breakfasts and church services. It had all happened before most Christians were stirring and long before most of the world was even awake. My life's most memorable moment came a few years later when I personally received Christ in a nearby church, but the brief broadcast was filed away for important reference.

For several Sunday mornings, at Dad's invitation, we had driven the fourteen miles from Baldwinsville to the downtown Syracuse radio studios of WSYR, he to sing and I to watch. I waited in the lobby, looking through the slanted, double-paned glass separating curious visitors from gifted performers. That morning, Dad said, "You can come inside, but don't you dare laugh, cough, sneeze, talk, or shuffle your feet." Although I had no intention of ever making any of the forbidden sounds, a sudden fear gripped me that all of them would somehow happen at once. But if Dad would trust me, I would risk it. We walked into the studio where programs really happened.

Thankfully, none of those distractions occurred while I sat alone on the risers at the far side of the studio watching the pastor preach, the quartet sing, and the cool-headed engineer brood over his many intriguing gadgets in the tiny control room.

The actual broadcast was brief. Its impact, although indistinct at the time, was permanent. I had witnessed a live radio broadcast. I had observed five early risers who loved their Savior more than sleep. More personally, it was a heady encounter with Dad's living testimony, a vital Christianity without veneer, a Christianity willing to rise early, to use precious gas during the rationing war years so he could serve the Lord and reach the lost. During that indelible Lord's Day broadcast, it had dawned on my impressionable young mind that the miracle of radio had sped the essence of their devotion to an unseen and unnumbered central New York audience. My vision for a radio ministry began that morning when I was ten years old.

Twenty-five years after that Sunday morning excitement, "The Word and the World" radio program began on nearby WMHR–FM from a high hill on the outskirts of Syracuse, a significant expansion of our growing radio ministry. In addition to its own powerful signal, that single station multiplies our outreach through ten translators, a college campus station, and across Lake Ontario to the Kingston, Canada, cable system. Today, WMHR is one of thirty-three outlets airing "The Word and the World," a program of biblical commentary and interview.

An interim boost between that first inspiration and its later implementation came from radio ministries at Northeastern Bible College when live "Morning Meditations" and Sunday evening broadcasts originated from the school. During my five-year pastorate following graduation, the Reverend Paul Anderson returned from an evangelistic crusade in Costa Rica and asked my help to fulfill a promise he had made to begin a follow-up radio ministry. We produced broadcasts which went into Panama and the British West Indies, as well as Costa Rica.

In 1956 I left my pastorate to establish Dedication Evangelism, declaring in my resignation message that I would be "dividing my time between . . . presenting the Lordship of Christ in local churches and gospel broadcasting which can reach millions in minutes." However, it was not until 1964 that the dream of "reaching millions in minutes" became a reality. While conducting evangelistic meetings in a small Pennsylvania town, the host pastor asked me to speak for two weeks on a free daily program shared by the local ministerium and aired on the town's single commercial AM station. Every listener could hear only that station because of the town's relative isolation and the towering hills. I assumed that Christians would seize this fantastic evangelistic tool which could effectively reach such a captive local audience. The pastor had no broadcast enthusiasm but at my urging he inquired about the station's rates. Not even the super bargain of fifty cents a minute changed his mind. I suspect that in his boyhood his father had never taken him to an early morning live radio broadcast.

Several months later, my personal negotiations with the station were finalized. On Sunday morning, April 12, 1964, the first broadcast of "The Word and the World," then a half-hour program, was aired over WFRM, in Coudersport, Pennsylvania. The thirty minutes cost $12.60, less than 50¢ a minute, a stupendous bargain. It began at 7:30 A.M., about the same time that the six of us had watched the second hand sweep toward air time twenty years earlier.

Or were there seven in the studio that early Sunday morning in 1944? Jesus reminded His followers that where two or three gather in His Name, He would be there. Six of us had met in Jesus' name in the context of early morning live radio evangelism to fulfill His command to "Go into all the world." By faith, godly men have always seen and obeyed "Him who is invisible," as Hebrews 11:27 states. I saw only those who saw Him. However, through them, God was lighting a fire in my heart that would still burn long after the igniting spark had flickered out.

I didn't understand it then. I do now.

**Lynn and Judy Everswick and family**

# ~ 11 ~

# Peace in Peril

## Judy Everswick

*The Reverend Lynn Everswick, his wife, Judy, and their five children returned to the United States in August 1983 after fifteen years of missionary work with T.E.A.M. in Zimbabwe, Africa.*

*The Everswicks met as students at Northeastern Bible College. She graduated with a B.R.E. in 1967 and he with a B.R.E. and Th.B. in 1968. They were married soon after. Lynn grew up in a missionary family in Zimbabwe and was drawn back there for service, as have been his two brothers and a sister.*

*Lynn Everswick is now area foreign secretary for T.E.A.M.'s West Asia fields. He is the administrative liaison and pastor for T.E.A.M. missionaries in Pakistan, Nepal, India, Sri Lanka, and the United Arab Emirates. He helps work out special governmental and personnel matters related to his fields and assists in establishing field priorities and goals with respect to the overall aims of the total organizations. The Everswicks live near Wheaton, Illinois, location of the Evangelical Alliance Mission headquarters, and Judy continues to be a close partner in his important work.*

Looking back on lives punctuated with reminders of memorable encounters with God, we find it difficult to pick out only one incident that would characterize our relationship with our Savior. Our backgrounds are very different—Lynn being brought

up as a missionary kid in Africa and I as the daughter of a tug-
boat captain in New York Harbor—but each of our meetings
with Jesus was very precious.

Lynn's desire to return to the mission field came as a result of
seeing the need for people to serve in a cross-cultural situation.
He knew the people, country, and culture of Zimbabwe as well
as having learned the dialect of the people as a young child.
Seeing the joy and enthusiasm that his parents had in serving
Christ left him in no doubt that there could be no more challenging or fulfilling career for him than to return to the mission field.
As is the experience of many missionary kids, he had to work
through the question of whether he was returning to Africa just
because it was his homeland. Having wrestled with the answer
by asking God to close doors if he was returning for the wrong
reason, he received confirmation from God for service overseas,
and Lynn began his preparatory studies at Northeastern Bible
College.

After committing my life to Christ as a teenager, I was challenged at a HiBA Missions conference about the opportunities
for serving Christ overseas, particularly in Africa. I accepted
that challenge and began to make plans to prepare myself to go.
I had heard about Northeastern and sent an application for the
following fall. Lynn and I met during the first week of school,
began dating a few months later, and were married after graduation.

Our dream of going to Africa was realized when we boarded
a plane in June, 1969, just two years after we graduated from
NBC. Kim, our first child and only daughter, was two months old
at this time. Our first seven years in Africa were spent on a
mission station in a remote tribal trust land. Lynn's childhood
fluency in Shona, the dialect of the Chizizuru people, rapidly
returned and within months he was able to minister in a variety
of ways, including managing six African schools.

Shona came to me with ease as I cooked with, sewed with,
and made friends with the African women.

The war of liberation in Rhodesia was beginning to intensify
when we were assigned a new responsibility. With a certain

amount of apprehension we began a pastoral ministry in Bindura, a small mining and farming town. Part of our responsibility was church planting and outreach ministry in the farm and mine compounds where hundreds of Africans were living. It was challenging and the opportunities were abundant. There were many English-speaking white people in the town who had earlier expressed a desire for a Bible study. One class was started in the home of the missionary who was living there, and the group began growing to the point that it needed to move into a church for evening meetings. Lynn felt a distinct sense of inadequacy as he contemplated ministering in English to white people. After considerable wrestling over the issue with God, we accepted the challenge and began a new phase of pastoral ministry.

Serving there for eight years was one of the greatest periods of stretching and growing that we ever experienced, with new challenges presented on a regular basis. The world at large perceived the problems in Rhodesia to be "merely" racial tensions, i.e. black vs. white problems. Our work was with the two groups: white, English-speaking people; and black, Shona-speaking ones. Could two races, involved in a bitter, dragged-out war, begin to understand each other or, even more remote, love one another? How exciting it was for us to see, from first-hand experience, that Jesus is truly the Bridge Builder.

War-time seems to get people actively thinking about God. Is there such a Being? If there is a God, how could He allow such a thing as war? Can a person really have a personal relationship with God? When one of our mining friends, who was not a believer, was dressed in his combat uniform and ready to leave on a four-week stint of duty, I asked him if he ever thought about God? His response: "Yes, when I am in a foxhole under fire and I am wondering if I will ever see my family again."

With fighting and death so close at hand, people no longer had the luxury of sitting on the fence in their relationship with God.

Young men from both our congregations were called to defend their country, and many times it was against one another.

Sorrow and grief at losing a son in combat, or a daughter in a plane shot down by guerrilla bullets, or a child in an ox cart that hit a land mine differ not because of the color of one's skin or the language spoken. The pain and heartache were equally evident in the faces of the people as they sat in the pews of the old church during the English-speaking service or on the roughly hewn logs in a renovated horse stable at a Shona service on a farm in the country.

Our lives were challenged and blessed and will never be the same as we saw the difference that Christ made in the lives of women and men who made Christ Lord of their lives. For example, there was Reggie who worked as a foreman on a chicken farm. When God changed his life, despite painful arthritis, he would bike for miles to farms in the area to share Christ's love.

Alison, the wife of Reggie's employer, came to our door one day. "You don't know me," she said. "I am an atheist. I don't believe in the Bible or the organized church, but you hold church services on our farm compound. Reggie is our foreman, and he has something in his life that I don't have in mine. Please, could you tell me what it is."

Feeling that she would not be allowed to attend church immediately, Alison met in our home weekly for several months before she committed her life to Christ. The enthusiasm and love for Jesus Christ of a black farm laborer bridged the gap and ministered to a white farm owner, a memorable encounter with God!

Adrian was a handsome and tough Italian miner who took pleasure and pride in his times of combat, both in war-time experiences and in his personal life. When his wife, Pat, accepted Christ as her Savior, she prayed for his salvation. There were times in their marriage when many would say there were irreconcilable differences, but Pat chose to remain with him, hoping that her unbelieving husband would accept Christ if she would, by God's grace, continue to live a consistent life. After she had prayed and shared for seven years, he came to our door and said, "I have decided I cannot fight God any longer."

The list of God's victories in transforming lives of men and women can go on and on, each with its own unique story. As we recall each one, we are reminded of invaluable experiences with God as we learned to walk one step at a time, depending on Him for direction and guidance.

Highlighting our days in Zimbabwe was the birth of our four sons. Rick was born while we still lived in the tribal trust land and Bradley came shortly after we moved to Bindura. Two years later we were surprised to discover that God was going to give us another child. We sent letters to the grandparents in America to tell them that a caboose was to be added to the Everswick train. However, some weeks later, after a visit to the doctor, another letter had to be sent asking them if they knew the plural of caboose. The specialist confirmed that we were to have twins. If I ever doubted the complete sovereignty of God before, I certainly did no longer.

The news of the twins' coming spread rapidly throughout our community. Plans were made to expand our home and it became a community project. The merchants in our town were Greek and generous, giving people, but they had not participated in church activities. However, one family had had twins some years earlier and so there was now a special affinity with us. God used the twins as bridge-builders. Even their birth was a community project. Because of the road ambushes, we were not allowed to use any roads leaving our town after four in the afternoon or before six in the morning. Nevertheless, a crew of people was mobilized to give escort should it be needed for a nighttime trip to the hospital.

The war continued to intensify. Ambushes, landmine explosions, and attacks on farms were occurring with alarming regularity, and the frequency with which Lynn was called upon for funerals was tragic. Only a few months after he married one young couple, the bride being the daughter of the church chairman, he held a memorial service for the groom, who was killed in a road ambush. The son of another board member was killed shortly before celebrating his twenty-first birthday. On another occasion Lynn was called to our nearby hospital to help a family brought there by helicopter after being caught in crossfire. Each member of the family had been hit by bullets, and the four-year-old boy was fatally injured. As Lynn carried him to the morgue and saw how like our little Brad he was, his heart reached to God for a fresh blessing and touch from Him.

These were days when pat answers and the old clichés just would not work. But God had promised that we could call on Him in the days of trouble and He would give strength. Over and over as we talked with people and asked whether they were believers or unbelievers, they would respond that it was the love of God and His word that brought comfort. God did not fail us when our own words would not come. When our hearts felt like breaking with empathy, the presence of a living God filled the vacuum.

One night Lynn and I had to be at a school function in Bindura. Baba Friday, a faithful African man who lived on our property, agreed to check on the children. Our daughter, Kim, was eleven; Rick, eight; Brad, three; and the twins, Timothy and Brendon, just a year old. As parents, we had chosen not to emphasize the war, for the children heard more than their share about it at school and all around them. However, as we left that night, Lynn said to Kim, "If you should hear any loud noises, wake all the boys, put them in the hallway, and close the door. Then try to lie still until we get home." There had not yet been any attacks on the town as a whole, but rumor predicted them and Lynn wanted to prepare the children, without alarming them.

Shortly after ten that evening I finished serving the dinner at the school, and Lynn and I joined another couple to eat. Just then the noises began. I hadn't realized how loud mortars and machine guns could be until we were under attack and the town was surrounded. No one could leave the building and we had to lie on the floor under small tables.

The promise of Paul to the Philippians became real: "Do not worry about anything; pray about everything; don't forget to thank Him for the answers; when you do this you will experience a peace from God that the world knows nothing about" (Phil. 4:6–7, LB).

Could God provide that peace for a young girl who was watching her four little brothers? We felt the peace of God envelope us as we continued to pray under the table. Even more than for their safety, our prayers were that God would grant that the children would experience His peace too.

It was twenty minutes before Lynn could be escorted home on an army vehicle. As he entered the house and went into the hallway, five pajama-clad children lay asleep on their pillows in the hall. Kim woke up and said, "Daddy, can we go back to bed now?" There was no fear nor tears. In the midst of the booms and bangs, five little children had left their warm cozy beds, nestled down on the hard wooden floor, and fallen quickly back to sleep. They were enfolded in the arms of God and were experiencing "the peace of God that the world knows nothing about" and their parents, once again, had had a memorable experience with a God who loves us and cares for us on a day-to-day basis.

The end of the war brought great relief. However, the coming to power of the black Marxist government presented different challenges for both the white and black citizens of the new Zimbabwe. Could trust between the races be restored? What would happen to the economy? There had been such intense fighting for so many years that it was difficult to comprehend a complete reversal almost over night. Guns and ammunition were no longer an accepted way to solve the differences between groups of people. However, the language barrier still existed, and the cultural barrier was more noticeable than before. The government was being run by people with a different mind-set than before. Goals were different, as well as the way to achieve those goals. Different does not mean wrong but, nonetheless, not the way it was done in the past.

More than ever before, Lynn and I were excited about our ministry of being bridge-builders. But our five-year term had almost come to an end and we were expected to return to the United States on furlough. We had some misgivings about leaving at that time and received permission to delay our furlough one or two years. But after much prayer we decided to stay with our original schedule.

One of our mission's first requirements when missionaries arrive back in the States is for them to have physical examinations. The doctor pronounced Lynn in good health except that a large black spot on his neck should be removed. It was done and we thought no more about it. When I brought the children for their physicals a few days later, the doctor called me aside to tell me that Lynn's growth was a melanoma and that Lynn probably had a 25 percent chance of survival. He requested that I bring Lynn back later that day to discuss the situation.

Shaken, frightened, and bewildered, I told Lynn. His first words were, "Judy, God has never made a mistake in our lives. I am sure that He is not going to begin now. Healing is within His power if that is what He wants. But if He should choose to take my life, He will care for you and the children just as He always has."

Together we went back to those precious verses in Philippians and shared with God our needs. We once again experienced the peace of God that the world knows nothing about.

The second surgery was successful in removing all the cancerous cells. When I asked the doctor how much longer it would have have been until the tumor had spread to the lymph nodes, he replied that there was no sure way of knowing but that melanoma is fast growing and six months more would probably have been too late.

God doesn't make mistakes. If we had had our way and remained in the field another year or two, there is no way of telling the outcome.

Perhaps each of us has experienced times in our lives when we have felt stubborn and determined to do things our own way. Lynn had accepted three challenges from our field council of things that he never wanted to do: managing black primary schools; serving as houseparents in the mission hostel caring for the M.K.s; working with the white people in Bindura. However, taking on these challenges had produced our growth as a family, growth as individuals, and growth in awareness of the presence of God.

In 1982 Lynn was asked to consider the position of field chairman, which would mean leaving our ministry in Bindura and changing boarding schools for Kim. Contrary to the way he usually responded, Lynn asked that he not be considered and spent the next several months feeling miserable about his decision. In late December he said, with lighter heart than I had seen for some time, "Judy, I have settled the issue with God and feel I have learned a valuable lesson. If I am ever again in that position where I am told that men of God are challenging me to a task that I personally feel inadequate to fulfill, I know I want to trust God to work through me."

Lynn's newly found commitment was tested only two weeks later when Dr. Richard Winchell of T.E.A.M.'s international headquarters asked him to consider assuming the responsibilities of area foreign secretary for West Asia. This would mean leaving our beloved Zimbabwe. The decision involved me also. Hadn't God challenged me as a young girl to serve Him in Africa? We loved it there and He was blessing our ministry. Did God really want us to move?

Returning to serve in the States seemed to be the biggest sacrifice we had made for God. It took me several months of fighting my own personal battle with God until I finally surrendered to the change in opportunity and outreach. At last, with peace of heart, I said, "O.K. Lord, I promised you that I would serve you wherever, whenever, and however. Even if that now means in Wheaton, Illinois, I want to be used by you." It was another encounter with a loving God who doesn't make mistakes.

Our ministry still provides new vistas and challenges, equally as exciting as those that we experienced overseas, for people everywhere need the Savior. Reflecting on these past years, I feel that perhaps none of the experiences recounted were really momentous, but each one was influential on our lives. We look forward to more years of serving God and encountering Him on a daily basis.

**James and Judith Parlier
with a Ulithian language helper**

# ~ 12 ~

# God Sent Rain

## Judith Parlier

*With her husband, James, Judith Parlier has been a Wycliffe Bible translator since 1962, first in New Guinea and now on Yap in the West Caroline Islands. She was born in Newark, New Jersey, in 1938, and as a small child moved to Nutley, New Jersey, where she attended school.*

*Jim Parlier was born in 1936 in Elizabethton, Tennessee, and grew up on a farm, milking cows and feeding chickens and pigs each morning before catching the school bus. Through school he became involved in what is now CBM Ministries and at their summer camp learned about missions and missionaries. Before he left high school he made a commitment to the Lord. He went to Northeastern Bible College where he learned from a visiting speaker about the Wycliffe Bible Translators.*

*The Parliers had three summers of linguistic training and three months in the jungles of Mexico to prepare them for their work in New Guinea, which is described in the following chapter. They now are working on the Ulithian New Testament. Named Alumni of the Year by Northeastern in 1967, the Parliers have three children: Rick, born in 1964; Randy, in 1966; and Tanya Jill, in 1970.*

I have gone to church all my life. My mother enrolled me as an infant in the nursery of an Italian Baptist church and I was carried there, every Sunday without fail. As the years passed, I became active with the young people, never missing any activities at the church.

One summer, when I was eleven years old, our Sunday school class went to Harvey Cedars Bible Conference. On the first evening there we broke up into groups for Bible study. That night, for the first time in my life, I learned what it meant to be "born again." I had never heard the phrase before my counselor explained the meaning to me, and I realized that all my perfect attendance records at church and my good works meant nothing. Without having Christ as my personal Savior, trusting in His blood alone to make me righteous, I could not have the eternal gift of heaven. That night, July 7, 1951, I asked Jesus to come into my heart and life and make me His child.

In high school I became involved in a group called "Hi-School Born-Againers." There I was introduced to missions and various missionaries. And the fight began. I didn't want to be a missionary, yet something inside me was tugging at my heartstrings telling me that was what I should become.

Satan knew more than I did, and so he brought Johnnie into my life, knowing I would fall head over heels in love with him. Johnnie was of a different religion and didn't know Christ as Savior, nor was he interested in "that stuff."

Still I attended Hi-B.A. meetings every Thursday, but I felt guilty about being there. The group was praying that I would be convicted and break up with Johnnie. The pain of the conflict was searing, for I had never known such love, and Johnnie became my whole life.

"I love him too much to break up with him," I cried out to the Lord in prayer every day. Then once I prayed, "Lord, if you don't want me going with Johnnie any more, you must break it up for me. I'm too weak."

Not long afterwards the phone stopped ringing after Johnnie had stood me up on some dates. The climax came at a party my best friend gave. Suspecting nothing, I walked into the kitchen to refill my punch glass and there was Johnnie with another girl. Quickly I retreated to the living room where the other guests sat in silence, staring at me. Suddenly I realized everybody knew about Johnnie's other girl but me. Fleeing the house, I ran the five blocks to the privacy of my bedroom. I reached for the stuffed dog Johnnie had given me, hugged it close, and sobbed.

"The burning flames of hell couldn't be more painful than this," I thought, wishing for death to swallow me up. But God had other plans for my life.

Because I felt that I wasn't growing as a Christian at the Italian church, I began attending another church in Bloomfield, New Jersey. It seemed an exciting place to go. The music was wonderful, but it was the pastor, Dr. Charles W. Anderson, who intrigued me most.

At times he seemed to have no mercy as he preached, openly displaying little patience with those who didn't walk the straight and narrow road. "Is he made of steel?" I wondered as I sat in awe, usually in the last row of the church where his keen blue eyes couldn't focus on me so closely. However, at other times I saw warmth and love emanating from those same perceptive eyes. He made me laugh and cry, and the Holy Spirit used him to convict me of certain things in my life. Eager to learn something new about the Lord, I could hardly wait for the next service.

One Sunday night the dashing, gray-haired pastor with the rimless glasses was behind the podium saying, "This is your last chance. If you want to go to the best Bible school America has to offer, you have to get your applications in this week."

*Is this where you want me to go, Lord? Is this the next step for me?* I wondered.

"Come on you girls," Dr. Anderson urged, seeming to look straight at me. "This is a chance for you to catch a husband." The twinkle in his eye matched the elfish grin on his face. "Sign up now, before it's too late."

*Okay, Lord, I'll go*, as long as I don't have to be a *missionary*, I vowed inwardly.

Living in the dorm at Northeastern was like a little bit of

heaven. The school choir sang like angels, lifting me up to the sky. My roommate and I got along fine and we became closer than sisters. Later as Mrs. Pat Duke Williams, she went to Iceland as a missionary.

For the first time I looked forward to classes, ready to drink in all the teachers imparted to us. Chapels were my favorite time, each speaker giving us nuggets of gold from the Scripture to build us up in the faith. It wasn't long before these saints prepared me to say, "Yes, Lord, here am I, send me." *(As long as I don't have to look like a missionary, Lord, I'll go.)*

Because the Bible was the main textbook at Northeastern, it became very precious to me. The missionary work that appealed to me the most was to give God's Word to a Bibleless tribe somewhere in the world where there was no way for these people to read the gospel message. Wycliffe Bible Translators specialized in this task, and it was to this mission I applied, but not by myself.

What happened to the husband I was "supposed to catch"? It didn't take too long to do that. In fact, it was at the first Sunday dinner at Northeastern when I spied through the small window in the door that led to the kitchen a pair of fantastic blue eyes staring at me.

Then, to my surprise, Dr. Anderson came through that same door, heading straight for my table. Before I knew what was happening my chair was being pushed back and my dignified pastor had his hand on my arm half lifting me up out of my chair. He was wearing that mischievous grin I was beginning to know so well.

"Come with me, young lady," he said. "There's someone I want you to meet." I knew I would be confronting the handsome student who had been staring at me. He led me to the kitchen and into the back room where the owner of the fantastic blue eyes was trying to hide.

With his free hand he grabbed hold of the embarrassed, lanky boy with a brown crewcut and brought us face to face. "I want you to meet Jim Parlier," he said to me. Then to Jim, "Okay, Jim, the rest is up to you."

On June 6, 1959, my graduation day from Northeastern Bible School, Dr. Anderson pronounced Jim Parlier and me "man and wife." Before the night was over Jim and I were driving to Norman, Oklahoma, where we would be trained at the Summer Institute of Linguistics.

In February, 1962, we set sail for Papua, New Guinea. The Managalasi people, an isolated group living on top of a mountain ridge in the northern province, seemed just the people Jim and I felt called to serve. However, they were suspicious of us, not understanding why we would want to live among them. Perhaps we were after their land, they thought, or maybe there was about to be another war, since we were Americans. The last time they had seen Americans was during World War II.

But after watching us closely for a while, they decided the real reason we were there was that Jim was looking for another wife. The wife he had, they observed, never did any work; she didn't even know how to make a fire to cook food. All she did was write down designs on paper. Such a useless thing!

It was through the avenue of medicine that we gained acceptance from these people. We washed their sores, treated their ulcerated wounds, gave them malaria treatments, and they saw that they recovered much quicker than when they simply waited for nature to heal. Realizing that we weren't there to harm them, but rather to help them, they began to trust us.

When our first son, Rick, was born in 1964, they accepted us completely. They then welcomed us with outstretched arms whenever we visited them carrying Rick, who opened the door to their hearts. Our second son, Randy, was born during our first furlough. After a refreshing year in the States, we returned to New Guinea and the Managalasis.

The language was coming easier to me now and the Thursday night Bible studies with the women were well under way. They loved singing the hymns and memorizing the Scripture verses that Jim was translating with his helper, Poki. Prayer time, however, was more like a health clinic. Every request was related to sickness, aches and pains. They were sure it was the spirits attacking them and many came to be prayed for.

During our second term on the field one of the driest spells in memory occurred in the mountain range where the Managalasi people lived. It was six weeks into the wet season, but still no sign of rain. The spring where the people went to fetch water was just a little dribble. The soil in the gardens was parched hard, killing the roots of the plants that had been laboriously planted weeks before. The beautiful grass in the village turned an ugly brown, the banana trees drooped lifelessly beneath the scalding sun. The entire land was crying for water.

Thursday night came and I prepared to go to the Bible study. As I walked the narrow path that led from our house to the village, I gazed up into the sky filled with bright, twinkling stars. *Too bad,* I thought, *there's no sign of rain in sight. How will these people survive this year without food?* I continued on my way to Isoro's house, the assigned place for the study that night.

The meeting with the women began with the singing of hymns, as usual. Next came prayer time and I was writing down the names of all the sick people. Then Namiji, an older woman sitting in the back corner, spoke up, "Judy, pray for rain," she said. "If it doesn't rain soon our gardens won't grow and we won't have anything to eat. There'll be no harvest, we'll all be hungry." The rest of the women joined her. A chorus of people cried, "Yes! Pray for rain *tonight* so we'll have food to eat. Pray for the rain to come tonight!"

A new hope seemed to fill their faces as I sucked in my breath in horror. I had seen the clear night sky a short while ago and knew there wouldn't be any rain tonight. Standing in shock before all these brown-skinned faces with their eyes anxiously fixed on me, I sent up an S.O.S. to God, *Lord, what shall I do?* From out of nowhere the words floated to me, "And whatsoever ye shall ask, I will do it." So I prayed for rain to fall that night.

Even though I was certain it was meteorologically impossible, I had peace about praying for their gardens, that everyone would have plenty, that no one would go hungry, that God would send some rain "tonight, Lord."

When I looked up after the prayer was finished, everyone seemed satisfied and settled back to hear something from God's

Word. Ten minutes passed and I was well into the message when the sound of light raindrops on the thatched roof was heard. The roof was old and wilted from the sun, and soon the rain was pouring through the many holes. Large drops spattered in the windows. The atmosphere in the room changed from a quiet calm to chaos. The women were crying, hugging each other, and calling out that the rain was here! Men's voices yelling excitedly to each other filled the air outside.

A feeling of happiness such as I had never known overtook me. I sensed the presence of the Lord with us in that broken-down house. I could only pray for the Holy Spirit to make my thanks known to the Lord, for I knew no words to express my complete joy.

"Judy! Judy!" The women were calling my name and I was jolted back into reality. "Don't talk to us anymore. Stop what you're saying from God's book! We all want you to stop talking." Namiji explained, "All of us in this room want you to pray again and thank God for giving us this rain. Tell Him that we say 'thank you' for helping us."

And so again we all bowed our heads humbly before God and thanked Him, not knowing that this was only the beginning of the miracle for the Managalasi people.

Every person, young and old, knew that it was God who caused the rain to fall that night. It wasn't the result of the magical purple plants they had laid around their gardens, nor was it Loturi, the rainmaker. This was big news on the grapevine, and soon word reached all the Managalasi villages on both sides of the mountain. And many, especially those who never attended Bible study, acknowledged in their hearts that there was a true and living God high in the sky.

And so, for more than a decade, we continued our ministry to the Managalasi people, in witnessing and Bible study and medical service, all the while steadfastly working on a Bible translation, our major purpose.

Finally, in 1976 the Managalasi New Testament was in the hands of the printer in Hong Kong. Jim and I waited eagerly in the village for news to reach us that the book was ready and being sent to our headquarters in Ukarumpa.

Early one morning in May the exciting message was relayed to us via two-way radio. "Jim," the radio operator said. "Five hundred New Testaments are being sent out to you today. The plane should arrive about 9:30 this morning; would you be able to meet the pilot and help him off-load?"

Sonalu was in the house when we heard the news. She was fourteen years old when we first arrived and had helped us with language learning, teaching her own people to read, and was the first Sunday school teacher. Now she watched Jim get the motorbike out for the ride on the narrow dirt path to the airstrip a mile away. She waited until he was almost ready to take off and burst out, "Can I go with you?"

"Sure," Jim's reply was quick. "Hop on." I waved good-bye to them as they passed by the kitchen window. Sonalu was sitting behind Jim clutching tightly to his shirt as they disappeared around the bend.

Waiting at the airstrip Sonalu heard the plane long before Jim did. At 9:30 A.M. the single engine Cessna buzzed over the top of the strip and circled around for the landing. After exchanging greetings the pilot and Jim set to work unloading box after box of New Testaments.

Finally Jim could stand it no longer. He had to see what one of the books looked like. He tore open a box and pulled out a copy bound in dark blue vinyl. Immediately he began scanning each page. Were the margins correct? Any mis-spelled words? Were all the pictures in the correct spaces? Then he felt someone's eyes boring into him. He looked up and saw Sonalu staring back at him earnestly, trying at the same time to get a glimpse of the book.

"Can I see it?" she asked, her eyes pleading. Jim responded by placing the book in her eager hands. When she took it she didn't open the book. She wasn't interested in looking at the pictures or checking for errors. Instead she held the book to her bosom and gently caressed it. Then she began rocking it back and forth as if it were a baby. Her eyes were closed and her lips were moving. Jim strained to listen. Then he heard the words clearly,

"Thank you, Jesus, thank you, Jesus," over and over again. Tears of joy fell over her brown cheeks. Sonalu's reaction to receiving God's Word in her own language made all of Jim's struggles worthwhile—the malaria he suffered, the times of separation from his children, the frustrations of waiting for his translation helper to come and then to learn later he went off hunting, the times there weren't enough money to get supplies. To see someone loving God and loving His Word because of his being there was a translator's dream come true. A major work was completed.

For the past few years we have been working on the Ulithi New Testament. This required us to move to another island. Obtaining permission to live there was not easy. Ulithi is a closed society and no outsiders are allowed; even tourists are discouraged from visiting. When news reached us that the Ulithian people voted 100 percent to have us live on their island of Magmag, our hearts went up in praise to God who had answered the prayers of many and opened the door.

In April, 1987, the Gospel of Mark was completed and checked by the Translation Committee. The first book of the Ulithian New Testament about to be published is a cause of praise. Matthew has now been finished and Luke is at the stage of being checked. We are on our way to completing another New Testament and praise Him who supplies our needs.

**Samuel G. Simpson**

# ~ 13 ~

# Under His Direction

## Samuel G. Simpson

*Pastor Samuel G. Simpson has served in New York City as a home missionary of the Home Mission Board of the Southern Baptist Convention since 1966. In 1972 he was appointed pastor–director of Southern Baptist work in the Bronx. He has been the pastor of the Bronx Baptist Church since its inception in 1964, and simultaneously has pastored the Wake–Eden Community Baptist Church since 1972.*

*He has served as president of the East Tremont Church Community Association, president of the Bronx Division of the Council of Churches of the City of New York, president of the Council of Churches of the City of New York (1981–83), president of the Baptist Convention of New York (1986–88), president of the Bronx Shepherd Restoration Corporation (1985–88), moderator of Metropolitan New York Baptist Association (1979–81), vice president of Twin Parks Urban Renewal Association, secretary of Community Planning Board #6, member of the 46th Precinct Community Council, and member of the Board of Governors of Northeastern Bible College.*

*Recipient of awards and mentions from the Maryland Baptist Convention, he was the 1974 Alumnus of the Year of Northeastern Bible College, was mentioned in* Who's Who in Black America, 1975–76, *was cited as Clergyman of the Year by the Bronx Division of the Council of Churches of the City of New York, received an award of excellence in 1981 from Air Jamaica, and is mentioned in the 1985 edition of* Dictionary of Caribbean Personalities in Britain and North America. *In 1976 he received the*

*Distinguished Service Award from the Council of Churches of the City of New York.*

*Pastor Simpson has hosted several radio and television programs and has had articles published in newspapers and magazines, including the* Baptist World Journal.

*His hobbies are photography and reading. His motto is Psalm 37: 4. Pastor Simpson has traveled widely and preached in North and South America and Hawaii; in England and several European cities; and in Africa, Israel, Greece, Egypt, and India.*

---

One of the things that amazes me as I grow older and look back over my life is the fact that before I had a personal encounter with Jesus Christ it was my desire to be a preacher. Wondering how this could be, I used to attribute it to the environment in which I was born and raised. However, I have come to believe that it was God's plan for my life because, although I could not say why I wanted to preach, there was an inner urge that motivated my desire. Finally, the truth of this desire was made clear when I read Jeremiah 1:5: "Before I formed thee in the belly I knew thee and before thou camest forth out of the womb I sanctified thee and ordained thee a prophet onto the nations."

On December 6, 1931, I was born on the island of Jamaica, West Indies, to Luther and Mary Simpson. My father was a planter who served as district constable and associate secretary of the Cooperative Loan Bank of the district. He was an active church member and a deacon of the Gibraltar Baptist Church. My mother, a housewife, was also active in church work. It was therefore incumbent on me to attend Sunday school and all church services, except prayer meeting. This exception was allowed because we lived some distance from the church. However, prayer was never neglected in the home. The light of the family altar burned day and night. Sometimes as a child I resented this strict observance.

I attended the Gibraltar Preparatory School from age four to seven, age seven being the required age to enter primary school then. Because of my early preparatory training, I was given two years seniority, which placed me in the upper class of the lower school. Although school was very competitive, I managed to maintain a high standard and was selected by the headmaster to prepare for the First Jamaica Local Examination. I subsequently sat for the Second and Third Jamaica Local Examinations. For two years I was a monitor in my school.

During my last year in primary school I gave my heart to Jesus Christ. It was in a small mission where my mother gave the message and the altar call. I responded to Christ as the hymn "Where He Leads Me I Will Follow" was being sung. After being counseled and attending the enquirers class for several weeks, I was baptized in 1948 in the Gibraltar Church. I immediately became involved as a Sunday school teacher, a member of the choir, and in other church activities.

The boys and girls who played on the streets on Sunday afternoons interested me. I spoke about them to a friend and together we started a Sunday afternoon Bible class with four boys and girls. In less than six months we were teaching approximately forty children. This group was taken over by the Barnstaple Anglican Church when I had to leave for Kingston for further studies.

I entered the West India Training College and sat for the Cambridge Local Examinations in 1952. During my studies at the college I was head boy of the school and leader in other social groups for two semesters. I was vice president of the school's Christian movement and spoke on several occasions at other schools and Christian movements. It was during this period that I took up photography as a hobby.

After graduation I worked in the Jamaica Civil Service in the Treasury Department for four years. As I traveled across the island in the course of my work, I felt God's call to the ministry and prayed to know His will. I felt His leading.

Soon after leaving home for Kingston, I had transferred my membership to the Christ Church (commonly called the Jones Town Baptist Church) where the late M. E. W. Sawyers was pastor. I discussed with him my entering the ministry, and he advised me to continue in prayer and to follow God's leading. My parents and other Christian friends encouraged me. The following year I applied to the Calabar Theological Seminary but was told by the admissions committee to get some more preaching practice and re-apply the following year. I did not find this a disappointment because I was aware of God's guiding hand in my life.

My application to the Emmaus Bible School in Chicago was accepted, so I came to the United States in January, 1960. The school is a Plymouth Brethren Bible school and I did not like some of their teachings. Therefore after a year I went to New York where I started extension classes at the New York Theological Seminary, and took a course in professional photography at the New York Institute of Photography.

I was attending the Calvary Baptist Church in New York where Dr. Stephen Olford told me about Northeastern Bible School. In 1962 I became a fulltime student there. Soon afterwards, I met the Reverend David Morgan, a Jamaican who was assisting in the evening worship at Calvary Baptist Church.

After one service I spoke with the Reverend Morgan and he invited me to attend his church in Brooklyn, a new venture of the Brooklyn YMCA under the auspices of the Southern Baptist Convention. After attending for a few weeks, I saw a great need. The enthusiasm of the few people was contagious, and so I became a part of the fellowship. Visiting in homes in the community was one of the greatest challenges of my life.

During the summer of 1962 a number of us from the church, joined by Southern Baptist summer missionaries, surveyed over one thousand homes and apartments. I discovered the reality of so many lost people in the midst of so many churches, of so much poverty in the midst of affluence, and of racism as a factor to be dealt with. The poor housing was also appalling. I have never forgotten the experiences of that summer.

As I look back now, God was showing to me what was ahead. I could not see it then, but He was leading to my ministry in the Bronx.

Late in 1962 I met an old friend, Miss Lola Campbell and, after "casting the fleece before God," there was no question but it was God's will that we should be together. He was leading again. And so in July of 1963 we were married. God has graciously blessed us with two girls and one boy, Erica, Stephen, and Kim.

Some experiences in my life show how God will provide if we trust Him. Sometimes little evidences of His care are even more exciting than big ones. I was attending school in New Jersey and planning to be married. We had contracted with a photographer for wedding pictures but did not know where the money would come from to pay all the bills. A few weeks before the wedding a photographer friend came to see me and offered to take all the wedding photographs and put them in an album as a gift. However, we would need to pay for any photographs we would need for the members of the bridal party and our parents.

I immediately called the first photographer who agreed to cancel his contract. On the day our friend brought our album and the additional photographs, we did not have the money for the extra pictures, but we promised to pay the following week. When Lola and I arrived at church the next morning, there was a letter waiting for us from someone whom we had met only casually. It contained a check for the exact amount we owed the photographer. To us it was a special gift from God.

Many similar experiences occurred during this period, verifying God's call, direction, and provision for both of us.

In September, 1963, I was ordained to the ministry, and I now gave more of my time to First Baptist Church in Brooklyn, which by this time was established in a proper church building and was growing rapidly. My wife and I served there in several capacities until November, 1964, when we were commissioned to serve in the Bronx as missionaries, our first venture in church planting.

I continued to attend school, and in 1966 I graduated from Northeastern Bible College with a Bachelor's degree. I continued studies at New York Theological Seminary where I obtained a Master's degree. In addition, I took courses at Bronx Community College in administration, and other graduate courses at Union Theological Seminary and the Jewish Theological Seminary in New York.

We started the Bronx Baptist Church in 1964 as a Bible study.

We obtained a permanent home for the church with the aid of the Home Mission Board of the Southern Baptist Convention. It was a small two-family house that had been used as a Jewish Synagogue.

From the beginning we knew that we had to become involved with the community, and so we organized neighborhood visitation and attended all sorts of community meetings.

In 1966 the mission was incorporated as a church with ninety members. The ministry grew so rapidly that we desperately needed a larger building. In April, 1970, we moved into our present building at 331 East 187th Street. The present membership of the church is more than five hundred. In addition, Bronx Baptist has formed two other active churches, three missions, two day care centers, and a number of other ministries. I will describe briefly these churches and ministries.

The Community Protestant Church of Co-op City, started in 1971, is an interdenominational ministry in the most densely populated area in New York City, Co-op City. Co-op City has a quarter-million people of all nationalities. The church has more than three hundred members and is active in its outreach program.

The Wake-Eden Community Baptist Church, in the northeast section of the Bronx, was started in 1972. Today it is one of the most active churches in the area. It started the Wake-Eden Christian Academy, which serves eighty children daily. It operates an active after-school remedial program, has an outreach to several nursing homes and prison ministries, and sponsors a number of home Bible studies. The membership at Wake-Eden is more than 225, with a larger attendance every Sunday. In 1979 the property was purchased by the church, which is now making plans for expansion both of the church building and of the school.

Honeywell Baptist Chapel is situated in one of the poorest areas in the Bronx. It meets on the first floor of the two-family house originally occupied by the Bronx Baptist Church.

Castle Hill Baptist Mission meets in a home in the southeast section of the Bronx. This area is developing fast, with many high-rise apartment buildings and two-family homes. Condominiums are expected to come in soon.

The Grace Baptist Chapel meets in rented quarters in the North Bronx. It promises to be an aggressive ministry, reaching all classes of people.

Bronx Baptist Church is affiliated with the New York Baptist Association, the New York Baptist Convention, and the Southern Baptist Convention. Until 1970 its location was in an underprivileged area. Although it has moved in order to obtain larger accommodations, still it is an inner city church. For this reason it has geared its ministry to people existing under the severe tension of inner city life. Besides proclaiming the gospel and having the usual teaching and social ministries, Bronx Baptist is involved in the socio-economic life of the people. It works to obtain for the helpless and inarticulate such amenities as better housing, schools, and medical care, and improved sanitation. The Bronx Baptist Church was a founding member of the Twin Parks Association which was formed in 1967 for the primary purpose of sponsoring new housing for the community. Some twenty-two hundred units of housing have now been completed. The Bronx Church used its opportunity to distribute more than three thousand Bibles to new tenants.

Bronx Baptist Church is also part of the Bronx Shepherds Restoration Corporation, whose basic concern is the restoration of the total man in his environment by providing housing, employment, economic development, and the renewal and revival of churches in different communities of the Bronx. The ministers who comprise the Bronx Shepherds believe that the people of God must play a vital role in community renewal. The solution is not just new and renovated housing, but new and motivated people; not just employment, but employment with a purpose.

The people comprising Bronx Baptist Church are deeply conscious of the missionary purpose of the church and seek under God never to lose sight of this urgency. Theirs is the story of the faith and prayers of a handful of people who shared a vision, of their toil and sacrifice, their fasting and prayer and vigils. The Holy Spirit has blessed and used their willingness and obedience. We are confident that God will continue to work His purpose out. We are under His direction.

**Steven and Angela Leuice and family**

# ~ 14 ~

# The Devil Is Real

## Steven R. Leuice

*The Reverend Steven and Angela R. Leuice are missionaries
serving with Liebenzell Mission International in the western Pacific. Because of the turbulent times there now, they have asked
that their location not be specifically identified.*

*Both were born into Christian families, Steven in Ridgewood,
New Jersey, in 1958, and Angela in Portland, Indiana, in 1955.
Both received Christ as Savior as little children. Angela's parents
were missionaries serving in the area where she and Steven now
work. She attended the Faith Christian Academy in the Philip-
pines. On tour with her family she met Steven who was planning
to attend Northeastern Bible College. He persuaded her to go
there also. They were married as students in 1977 and graduated
with degrees of Bachelor of Arts in Biblical Literature in 1978.
They went on to study at Wheaton College and in 1980 both
received their Master's degrees in Communications.*

*The Leuices now have three children, Jessica Robin, age 7;
Kurtis Elisha, age 5; and Kirstin Melissa, age 2. Currently Steven
is the Liebenzell Mission director for the Theological Education
by Extension (T.E.E.) program in their island area. Their assignment includes major responsibility in a local church, with itiner-
ant schedules of preaching and teaching in surrounding villages,
some reached only by small boat. They are establishing a local
Christian radio ministry in association with one of the well-
known radio networks.*

"The Americans have not left. They are being watched. You choose to put them in danger. I only wish to warn you. I do not want harm to come to these people. My life too is in danger. There will be violence to your people next time the power is out. There is a plan of taking a person from Emmaus. You know these people do not play. They have guns and bombs. They have plans to destroy your houses. Do not wait for someone to be hurt. I will not send another warning. You will see what I say is true."

It was the second threatening letter we received during the week. The first one gave us one week to leave. Was it a prank of some sick joker? Who could tell?

In the years we have spent here we have come to know, respect, and love the islanders. Most are good, even friendly people. But in every society there are always a few troublemakers. In light of the recent bombings, attacks, murders, and political upheaval, we could not disregard the notes. We had to take precautionary measures. "Take it to the police," said one friend. "But how can they help us?" said another. "All we have are two anonymous letters."

The threatening letter was not the first time we met with Satan's opposition. The moment we first stepped off the plane we encountered the enemy. A new beachhead was being established and Satan didn't want to open up another front. When we arrived on the field, I thought Satan was an abstract force, a vague figure who pops in and out of the pages of Scripture. Then we met his cohorts face to face. This educated, scientifically oriented missionary began to understand the fear that grips the heart of every animist for whom the world of the spirit is as real as the mud between his toes.

Once we were visiting a small village and were treated to the hospitality of a national in her small house. A room was provided for us and the baby. With one bed and two mats, we were comfortable, until we were hit with the frightening reality that we were not alone. Like Elisha who was surrounded by his enemies at Dothan, we realized we were surrounded by a nefarious host. We could hear their footsteps as they marched around just outside the room. Huddled together, we trembled at the sound of their muffled voices. The air was filled with more than the humidity and our own perspiration. It was the foul smell of rotting dead flesh. As that evil presence enveloped the room, we prayed until we fell asleep with the enemy still encamped around us.

The first round was over; we had engaged the enemy and come out alive. We were green recruits, more like Elisha's servant than his master who, seeing God's angels, prayed, "Do not fear, for those who are with us are more than those who are against us" (II Kings 6:16). What we didn't know was how soon basic training would continue.

Back at our station, it wasn't long before Satan knocked on our door again. Actually, he was not quite so polite. I got out of bed to investigate eerie screams, half-human, half-animal, coming from the kitchen. Finding nothing, I was returning to the bedroom when all of a sudden I was pushed aside in the doorway. I struggled to enter the room. Inside, I pressed with all my strength to close the door. We prayed and with a shriek the demon fled from the house. Round two was over. We took the advantage.

I felt good now, much stronger than I really was. The next fight, I picked. I went to "counsel" a man reportedly "demon-possessed." Naively I went along with only my "sword," but was held at bay for what seemed like an eternity as this gentleman held a twelve-inch kitchen knife to my throat. Sobered, but not beaten, I decided it would be best to wait for an order to come down from the command headquarters before engaging the enemy again.

Shortly after that I spent two long days with a young demon-possessed man. He came from a long line of shamans. I agonized for him as he literally writhed in bed from the torture of his black prince. I felt no fear this time, only great pity. By this time Satan had become a real enemy and "spiritual warfare" no longer an academic discussion.

Do these accounts surprise you? This is not the product of an over-worked imagination. Satan's *modus operandi* in the West is to establish intellectual skepticism about his existence. Most everywhere else he has another tactic: *fear*. This tactic is successful, but although Satan has a frightening roar, he has no bite. His teeth were knocked out at Calvary! He tested us to see if we would run. By the grace of God we did not. But neither did he give up.

One of Satan's main targets on our field is the family. I suppose it has been that way ever since the Garden of Eden, and it is true all over. It just seems especially true for our field. Infidelity was rampant, wife-beating common. Unwed mothers abounded. A large percentage of children were being reared by someone other than their natural parents, passed around within the extended family, creating great feelings of insecurity. Discipline was frequently only verbal or abusive. With so much change going on, arranged marriages were becoming fewer and fewer. But no substitute was employed. Young people seen only talking together were assumed guilty of sleeping together. Our hearts were breaking over these broken homes. Satan, it seemed, was working overtime to disrupt family life.

We decided it was time to address the problem. We planned a T.E.E. course dealing with marriage and the family. We conducted seminars dealing with solving conflicts in marriage. Youth sessions dealt with finding a mate. Our sermons decried immorality and infidelity. We were taking a stand for the Christian home, when Satan raised his ugly head in ours.

We were married three years when we came to the field and had been friends twice that long. We brought a baby girl with us and two years later a son was born. If anyone could say theirs was a marriage made in heaven, we could. Yet it's easy to turn that kind of heaven into hell.

It happens little by little, like a cancer that secretly spreads unnoticed until it becomes serious. Through different opinions, harbored resentments, lack of appreciation, and uncontrolled tempers, Satan subtly entered our home and we didn't notice it.

Missionaries face some peculiar family problems. For one thing, husbands don't usually go off to work. My desk is in our bedroom. Frequently the missionary's work comes home to him: unscheduled business meetings in the living room, people calling for counseling, Bible studies on the porch, social gatherings everywhere. A missionary has enough jobs for ten people to do, but no one to help with the children while both the husband and wife do the ten jobs.

Moreover, there is very little social entertainment available on our island, nowhere to get away to for a few hours. On top of it all was the pressure of trying to adapt to a foreign culture, teaching our own children, living without all the nice little conveniences, and the embarrassment of being a cultural "infant" in a grown-up body. Then there were things like being an alien in a foreign land, droughts, unheard of illnesses, unbearable heat and humidity. It was easy for us to lose our cool.

Why do husbands and wives vent their anger and frustration on the one they love the most? Satan is surely a participant in spiritual warfare on the home front. While we were trying to build up other families, ours was deteriorating. Fear did not work. Satan's frontal attack was repelled. But the back door into our family proved to be weak and allowed him access. One time my wife reported to a ladies' Sunday school class that they should pray for missionaries' family life. It wasn't long before the pastor heard a rumor that we were on the edge of divorce. We had many laughs over that.

Things eventually improved. I believe the bottom line was simply the commitment to hang tough. Secular marriages don't have the cement it takes to bind a couple for life. When things in the home become unglued, the first talk is of permanent fracture, not of repair. Christian couples work things out because there is no other option. The trials really do make us strong. They purify us from self-centeredness. We learn to love as Christ loves—unconditionally. Satan had come in the back door. It took us a while to notice his infiltration, but, praise God, he was booted out again!

A wise old angler showed me his tackle box once. It was full of all kinds of lures of different colors and dimensions. He knew what type of lure would attract which kind of fish. Satan is like that. When one kind of bait fails to catch the individual, he simply pulls out another.

Many missionaries are independent, strong-willed visionaries with a touch of the entrepreneur's insatiable thirst for success. But the greatest frustration of most missionaries is conquering that seemingly insurmountable language barrier. Sadly, sometimes there is more competition than support from other missionaries in scaling the language barrier.

Moreover, the naive presumption that another missionary shares the same vision, goals, commitment, and spiritual maturity as his colleagues, that his fellowship will be similar to that of a high school retreat is utter foolishness.

Then there are frustrated ambitions. Nothing turns out quite like they said it would in orientation class. A missionary can scrap his job description, too. He goes with what works, and far too often the "harvest" is not what he expected. Satan will plague a missionary with feelings of failure and make him doubt his call.

Satan struck again. This time it was psychological warfare— real none the less. Through the study of Christ's parable about the day laborers in Matthew 20, I came to understand that Satan is the father of lies. He would have us measure our success in terms of the result produced.

God has a different measuring stick. In God's kingdom success is related to faithfulness, not to the outcome. The laborers who worked only one hour in the late afternoon received the same reward as those who worked the long hours through the heat of the day because they had been faithful to the limited opportunity provided them.

The Lord taught me that success is simply being obedient to the revealed will of God, nothing more, nothing less. The housewife who raises three children to the glory of God will one day receive the same reward as Billy Graham who has led thousands to faith in Christ. If both have been equally faithful to the revealed will of God, both will share equally in the reward.

I came to realize that I could be a success, no matter how I felt. In terms of success, results didn't matter—faithfulness did. We all have equal opportunity to strive for greatness to the glory of God.

With the issue settled, we began to see more tangible results than we had ever anticipated. It seemed as if there were signs of spiritual awakening. People were coming to Christ at every meeting. God was doing "a new thing and we could perceive it" (Isa. 43:18–19). Of course Satan counteracted with a new plan as well.

I recall one missionary saying, "All I want for Christmas is a regular bowel movement." Fortunately, the Lord has granted me a strong constitution. If I don't recognize what comes on my plate, I've learned not to ask questions. Generally I've been blessed with good health. Unfortunately, that's not true of my wife.

It seemed as if she contracted every exotic ailment that came along. Once while we were still in Guam as Angela was recouperating from a Caesarian section, I left the house for a few minutes. When I returned, Angela was writhing from pain. I quickly handed the children to a neighbor, then half carried her to the car and sped to the doctor's clinic. He rushed her in an ambulance to the hospital. The surgeon was on hand to take her immediately to the operating room. All this time no one attempted a diagnosis.

As I sat alone in the waiting room, fears swept over me. Would I be facing the future alone trying to raise a two-year-old and an infant? As I turned to the Lord, the fears fled, and the Lord reassured me with the words of a hymn: "When peace like a river attendeth my way / When sorrows like sea billows roll / Whatever my lot Thou hast taught me to say / 'It is well, it is well with my soul'."

My wife recovered and eventually encountered other types of sickness and pains. More than once we have had to leave the field for short periods for her to get needed medical attention. Even now, she suffers back pain that some days is only irritating, while at other times is excruciating.

Does the Lord know? Yes. Does He care? Yes. Can He heal her? Yes. If a doctor could heal someone, he would. God can, but sometimes chooses not to. Does that make God's sympathy any less than man's? No!

We don't see the reasons for sickness. We would rather have one piece of candy now than wait for a whole bag of candy tomorrow. But our Father in heaven loves us enough to see that we get the greatest blessing, even when it brings temporary pain.

Can Satan cause illness? Yes. Is he responsible for every illness? No. With God's child he can go only as far as our heavenly Father permits. This year six full-time church workers on our field were laid up because of the same back trouble. Was Satan up to his tricks again? Who can say with certainty. The ministry was certainly disturbed and the proclamation of the gospel disrupted. Satan was satisfied, whatever the cause.

We don't look for a demon behind every tree, but we do recognize we are in a spiritual battle. "For our struggle is not against flesh and blood, but against the rulers . . . against the powers of this dark world and against the spiritual forces of evil in the heavenly realms" (Eph. 6:12).

We have seen that "struggle" begin with power encounters with demons. We have seen the battle take place in our home, our minds, and our bodies. Today we face a terrorist threat. Two women took their children and left the country. We, along with other families, chose to stay. Policemen guard our homes at night. The U.S. State Department sent a telegram signed by George Shultz. The Admiral of the Pacific Fleet called and has "contingency plans prepared." We have the dubious honor of being Pacific front-page news.

Are we safe because of all this? No. We are safe only because we are in the arms of Jesus. We are as content as a nursing baby at its mother's breast because God is sovereign. We are excited because of the blessings we have already received. Through this small test we have been able to examine our own faith. We have the honor to love those who hate us and pray for those who persecute us. We've been drawn into deeper empathy for those who really suffer for the sake of our Savior. And we are expectant, as God's saints all around the world are praying down God's blessing upon this land.

**Jack and Faith Wilson and Faith Elizabeth**

# ~ 15 ~

# God's Creative Power

## Jack Wilson

*Jack Wilson grew up in a Christian home in Franklin Lakes, New Jersey. Through a high school youth group he was led toward full-time Christian work and followed his sister to North-eastern Bible College. He graduated with a B.R.E. in 1972 and took a postgraduate degree, M.Div, at the Biblical Theological Seminary in Hatfield, Pennsylvania. Then he became pastor of the Englewood (N.J.) Baptist Temple. He earned a M.Phil. at Drew University in Madison, New Jersey, and is currently work-ing toward a doctorate there.*

*During his years at Englewood, Wilson started a counseling ministry with the Reverend Kenneth Lont called Applied Biblical Counseling. The service is still operating but Mr. Wilson is not active.*

*In 1980 Wilson was called to the Calvary Evangelical Free Church in Essex Fells, New Jersey, as counselor and minister to college students. In 1982 he became senior pastor.*

*Pastor Wilson married Faith Touw in 1976, and they have a daughter, Faith Elizabeth, born November 10, 1980.*

---

In 1981 when my wife and I were living in Englewood, New Jersey, where I was serving a congregation of the Lord's people, we were expecting a child. Since Faith had previously had a miscarriage, we were now baptized into blood tests, and wait-ing and waiting and waiting, and more blood tests, and more waiting and then, Lamaze.

135

Lamaze is an amazing thing—almost religious in form. There is a special place for "Lamaze classes," as there is a special place for church. Couples who have similar commitments and goals meet together just as in church. We sat together in rows, just like in church. A Lamaze instructor acts something like a preacher or Bible teacher. She stands up front and gives forth the Lamaze doctrine. Everyone listens intently, just like in church. She shows a film once in a while, just like in church.

Then everybody breaks up into small groups, sort of like discipleship groups, only this part is not like in church, at least not in our church. The women all lie down. The husbands kneel next to them. What follows is the sound of rushing wind—breathing exercises. Then follow other kinds of exercises, but no "tongues as of fire." That all this is developed so that the husband can assist his wife in giving birth is truly an astounding concept when you think about it.

Of all the painful experiences God could have used as analogy, whenever He wanted to describe pain in the Bible, He said "pangs as when a woman travaileth." That God Himself views that kind of pain as severe ought to tell everybody something about the level of "assistance" a husband can give his wife as she "travails." Not much!

Anyway, we went through all that.

Towards the latter months of Faith's pregnancy, we found out about some complications. Unusual chemical changes were taking place, and her blood pressure had begun to rise. Her doctors directed that a closer watch be kept over her condition, and it seemed as if they tested her constantly.

About three weeks before her due date, we went in for more tests. We went to the out-patient service at Saint Barnabas Medical Center and, as usual, she disappeared and I waited. And waited. Longer than usual. Then a nurse walked into the room.

"You're going to be a father," she said.

"I know that," I replied.

"No, Mr. Wilson, you're going to be a father today!"

My first thought was *But we haven't finished our Lamaze classes!* I still thought that I was going to assist my wife in the birth experience, help her through the pain, help her bring the little Wilson into the world. My next thought was *Well, we probably know the basics.*

A few minutes later I was in Faith's room. When she had left me in the waiting area, she had walked away in her street clothes. Now, she was prone, plugged in, and dressed in one of those designer robes they give you in the hospital, that keep you warm in front and cool in back. All she told me was that the nurse had taken her blood pressure, had cried out, and had run out. The problem was toxemia.

The doctor arrived and we all agreed that he would try to induce labor. The inducement didn't do anything, which was disappointing, because we still believed in Lamaze. He then said, "We'll have to take the baby."

Returning from calling Faith's mother, I found that Faith had been wheeled away. I announced that I wanted to be with her and was told to wait. Well, I had had a lot of practice at that, but it didn't help. I prayed and paced and prayed and paced and then insisted that I be reunited with Faith. They dressed me in yellow, led me in to where she was, being incised for a Caesarean section. I watched as they finished, holding her hand.

That was a very strange time, a good illustration of faith. When the life of a loved one is in someone else's hands, there is really nothing to do except trust. It is then that one becomes very aware of Someone Else's Hand. And that Hand delivered a little baby. She was all red and tiny and wet and so very, very beautiful and so very much the creation of God Himself. The experience was overwhelming.

In the Bible, encounters with God usually brought about contrition, renewed conviction, and a new commission. It was no different for me when I received a girl child from the Lord. I was humbled. I had renewed conviction in the presence and power of God. And I definitely had a new commission, from God. "I have made her. I am entrusting her to you. I am giving you what you need to be the best father that she can have. And for her, you are accountable to Me."

I'd really appreciate your prayers. It's an awesome responsibility.

**James Bjornstad**

# ~ 16 ~

# A Modern-day Mount Carmel Experience

## James Bjornstad

*James Bjornstad is president of Northeastern Bible College. His is also professor of philosophy and theology. In addition, he is the executive director of the Institute of Contemporary Christianity, a research organization in Oakland, New Jersey, and an ordained minister.*

*Mr. Bjornstad married a Northeastern College classmate, Rebecca Ann Leonard, in 1967. They live in North Haledon, New Jersey, and have adopted twin daughters, now nine years old, Christine and Karen.*

*In addition to his formal training at Northeastern Bible College, New York Theological Seminary, and New York University, he has spent twenty-three years in religious research. A recognized scholar in the area of current religious movements, trends, and practices, Mr. Bjornstad has lectured extensively in colleges, universities, seminaries, and graduate schools, as well as in churches and conferences throughout the United States, Canada, and Europe. He has appeared on such television programs as "60 Minutes," "Hour Magazine," and the "John Ankerberg Show." He is the author of numerous articles for newspapers, magazines, and journals, and has written six books, including* Sun Myung Moon and the Unification Church *(Bethany House),* Counterfeits at Your Door *(Gospel Light), and* Playing with Fire *(Moody Press).*

*Mr. Bjornstad is a member of several educational and professional societies, including Delta Epsilon Chi and the Evangelical Theological Society. He has been included in* Who's Who in Contemporary Authors, Who's Who in the East, Who's Who in America, *and* Who's Who in Religion. *In 1973 he was named Northeastern's Alumnus of the Year.*

---

It was a beautiful day as I strolled through Greenwich Village on my way to my first class (Philosophy of Religion) of the new semester at New York University. A block or so from the classroom building, I picked up a container of black coffee and then continued on my way. After entering the building, I took the elevator to the third floor and walked down the hall to the designated room.

Several other students were already there, and so I opened my container of coffee and began to introduce myself to my fellow classmates. As I did this, I was especially intrigued by one man whom I shall call John. Whenever I would try to move toward him, he would move away from me. He was quite good at keeping a distance from me with people between us.

Finally the instructor entered the room and everyone found a seat. When I sat down, John chose the opposite side of the room, at the farthest point from me.

During the first session, the instructor asked us to introduce ourselves and say something about our present occupation and/or interests. I gave my name and told of my involvement with young people as minister of youth at the Van Riper–Ellis Memorial Baptist Church in Fair Lawn, New Jersey. I also told of my interest in researching religious movements and my work at the Christian Research Institute in Wayne, New Jersey, as assistant director of research. When John's turn came, he introduced himself as Brother John and said he was a messenger with the Church of the Final Judgment (also known as The Process).

This church was founded in London in 1963 by a former Anglican, Robert de Grimston. The essence of its theology centers around the existence of three warring deities: Jehovah, a stern god who demands obedience; Lucifer, who wants us to live life to the fullest; and Satan, who seeks to test us by offering evil as an alternative to good and to bring us down to a subhuman life of depravity. Christ is seen as our helper in this battle. He is the transcendent unifier who ultimately will reconcile all three gods.

How will Christ do this? According to Processeans, Christ has told us to love our enemies and therefore they believe that to overcome Satan, we must love him. Furthermore, if we are to develop ourselves spiritually, we must have contact with the great superbeings of the universe. For example, this contact is part of their Sabbath Assembly, their worship service on Saturday. It is also part of other services, such as their "telepathy development circles." John, as a messenger with this church, loved Satan and was in regular contact with spirit beings (demons).

During the next few weeks, I tried my best to meet John, but to no avail. In fact, on one occasion, when emerging from a subway station, I saw John across the street. I called to him and he turned and saw me. But instead of waiting for me as I crossed the street to where he was, he ran to cross the street so he would be on the other side from me.

One day in class the instructor, who loved to pick on me because of my beliefs, asked me to give the "fundamentalist" position on a certain issue. As I did, mentioning Jesus Christ and quoting from the Bible, I watched John hold his head with both hands and grimace, as if in pain.

The next week, John came to class dressed in his religious garb. His long black cape made him look like someone out of an old Dracula movie, but most noticeable was the decoration on his collars: a red, three-horned mendes goat's head and between the horns, a large silver cross (symbols of Satan and Christ).

Later that day, as I walked to the elevator, I saw John in one of the empty classrooms. I thought this might be a good opportunity to meet him. As I approached the room, I began to sense something I can only describe as heaviness. It was as if a heavy cloud (though invisible) was putting tremendous pressure on me. My head hurt and my heart was pounding. I entered the room and there on a table was a Ouija board with the pointer or "eye" moving by itself an inch or so above the board.

John stood with his arms folded on his chest and said, "Is your God as great as mine?" Before I could answer, he laughed and said, "Go ahead. Ask it any question." He laughed again and then said, "What is his mother's maiden name?" The pointer began to move and, letter by letter, spelled out my mother's full maiden name. He laughed again.

Frightened by all this, I prayed aloud and asked Jesus to "put an end to this demons' power." I prayed that Jesus would "cast this demon into that place He had reserved for him." The pointer dropped to the board, lifeless. John was shocked. To be honest, so was I. John flung the Ouija board across the room and ran out.

I never saw John again. Several years later, some former messengers of the Church of the Final Judgment told me that John was so bothered by me and by this encounter in which his superbeing was defeated that he requested a transfer to their church in Toronto. There he began a new search, I was told, for superbeings that were more powerful, with the intent of finding one that was greater than "Bjornstad's Jesus."

This has been the most memorable experience with God thus far in my life. Before then, I had known that Jesus and Satan existed and that prayer was powerful. However, that supernatural encounter brought a new dimension of reality to me, different from anything I had ever experienced before.

I will never forget it. It helped me to realize that Satan is alive and working today. It also caused me to realize the greatness of my Lord and Savior Jesus Christ, the importance of the Word of God, and of prayer.

**Moishe Rosen**

# ~ 17 ~

# The Almost Inaudible Voice

## Moishe Rosen

*Moishe Rosen is founder and executive director of the Jews for
Jesus ministry. He grew up in an orthodox Jewish home in Denver, Colorado. He and his wife, Ceil, also from a Jewish home,
were high school sweethearts and were married at age eighteen
as soon as they were graduated. They became Christians three
years later. When Moishe decided to train for Christian service,
they went east to Northeastern Bible College.*

*He graduated from Northeastern, and in 1957 was ordained to
the ministry. He was named Northeastern's Alumnus of the Year
in 1977.*

*Jews for Jesus is an evangelistic ministry to Jews. It has a staff
of more than one hundred people with six branches and fifty-six
chapters in the United States and Canada. It also carries on
short-term evangelistic campaigns in Europe, Australia, South
Africa, South America, and Israel.*

*Mr. Rosen has served as consultant on Jewish evangelism to
the Lausanne Committee on World Evangelism and to a number
of denominational evangelism boards. He has written five books,
some of which are required texts in Bible colleges and seminaries, and has contributed articles for major evangelical publications. He is a trustee of Western Seminary in Portland, Oregon,
and on the International Council on Biblical Inerrancy. He is
listed in* Who's Who in the West.

I had been a believer in Jesus for fifteen months before I entered Northeastern Bible College, and it had been a tempestu-
ous time. Because my wife and I were both Jewish, we had to go
through a great deal of reorientation to the Christian life. Not
only that, our families had not only disapproved of our decision,
but had disowned us, although there had been some reconcilia-
tion with my parents before we made the long trek to New Jersey.

I was a comparatively new driver and I was enjoying my new
used car, a five-year-old 1949 Hudson. Loaded into the trunk,
the back seat, and on the top was everything we thought we
would need during three years of schooling. My wife and I and
our young daughter set out on the pilgrimage from Denver, Colorado, to drive two thousand miles to Essex Fells, New Jersey. I
had never driven more than one hundred miles before, and so I
planned the trip very carefully. I made sure that the car was in
top-notch mechanical condition, that the load was secure, that
everything was working properly, and that there was oil and
almost new retread tires.

Every day of the journey was a time of excitement, just to see
this vast country from the highways. When we crossed the Mis-
sissippi Rover, we stopped at Hannibal, Missouri, and took a
boat ride.

After the joy of the busy days, I slept soundly every night until
we got to Columbus, Ohio. That night I could not sleep. Insom-
nia had never been a problem for me; I could sleep anywhere,
anytime. In fact, I have been inflicted with narcolepsy which, if I
am unmedicated, causes me to doze off. Until then I had never
spent a sleepless night in my life.

However, at Columbus, in a comfortable motel and tired after
a long day's drive, I could not go to sleep. It was as though a
Voice were speaking to me beyond my level of audibility, or as
though Someone were beckoning me beyond my sight. I knew I
should be trying to understand, but I was determined to sleep.
Even after counting three thousand sheep, I was still awake, and
an inner urge was insistent.

I got up, dressed, and searched in my automobile to find a
flashlight, never feeling a conscious impulse to get dressed or to

get out of the motel room, let alone to search for a flashlight. Then there came an inaudible Voice insisting, prodding, "Look under the car."

I knelt down, shined the flashlight under the car, and saw nothing. The Voice said, "Get down on your back." At 3:30 A.M. on the gravel driveway, I scooched around trying to find a position from which I could see.

The underchassis of the car was low to the ground, and I could see nothing wrong, but the feeling was insistent. I went back into the room, got the key, and backed the car up. Again I lay down, looking at the tires on the other side. Then I saw a huge, flat spot with broken strings in the beading and cording showing through the tire.

I lay there realizing what it meant. The following day I would have been entering the turnpike, driving at high speeds, and I knew that the tire would have blown out.

I can't predict what the outcome of such an accident would have been, but it could have been fatal. Certainly, I wouldn't have been able to start school on time. The one thing that was inevitable was that the tire was going to blow out.

I haven't heard that almost inaudible Voice many times, and I haven't seen an almost invisible Hand beyond the horizon beckoning me often, but it has happened on occasion. When it does, I believe it is God or His angels prompting me to discover what I otherwise couldn't know.

Another way in which the Lord dealt with me that year had to do with prayer. I had been a Christian for a year and a half and I did have a prayer life, but it was a prayer life of reading psalms aloud, praising God, and thanking Him for this or that. There was one important ingredient missing from my prayer life, and that missing ingredient was petition. At that time I could give what might have sounded to some like a good reason for never asking God to do anything, and I would have said, "I was satisfied with whatever I got and I would not ask for this or for that either for myself or anyone else."

Rather, I think that the truth was that I had a deep fear that the thing for which I might ask God would not come to pass. If it did not happen, I wouldn't have known how to handle it.

One has to understand that Jewish people have a certain kind of pride. For example, I was a Depression baby, but we didn't think of ourselves as being poor because no one else seemed to have much either. Nevertheless, when the conditions of the Depression seemed to ease, my father did not get a raise in salary (from twelve dollars per week), nor did he get a better job. As a consequence, we were still in the midst of a Depression when others were emerging. But I was told that when we went to visit our cousins, if somebody said, "Are you hungry?" I was always to say, "We just ate," which wasn't always true. Our meals at home were the monotonous food of those who were impoverished.

But to admit that our needs were not being met would have been a shame on my father as a provider.

My mother would rather starve then let anyone, particularly members of the family, know that my father was in any way inadequate in caring for the needs of the family.

Furthermore, we were conditioned not to ask anyone for anything, at any time, except for asking my mother who would have given us whatever she had. That might explain some of my reluctance at the petition part of prayer, but God was soon going to teach me His way.

My first semester at school found me in desperate straits. First of all, I had been out of school for three years and although I had done work on the university level before, the method of teaching and learning was very different in a Bible college. It required a lot of memory work and there was still some confusion in my own mind that did not plague the non-Jewish students. I had to unlearn a lot.

For example, they did not know about Avram, of whom I had learned many stories, although he was the same as Abraham that they were telling me about in my classes. I had learned a story of how when Avram was a boy working in his father's idol shop, his father, Terach, left him in charge. With a rod of iron, Avram smote and broke every one of the idols until they were rubble. When Terach returned and was stunned by what had occurred, he asked for an explanation, to which young Avram responded, "The idols got into a fight and destroyed each other." Terach rejected the obvious lie, pointing out that idols don't move nor do they fight, at which point, young Avram, said, "So, why do we worship them?"

You probably never heard that story before, unless you have studied the many legends of the Mishna, a Bible commentary in which the rabbis explain and enhance Bible characters. When I had identified Avram with Abraham, then I knew more than the other students and the teachers and was able to tell other such stories that they never heard. I was sure that it must be written in the Bible somewhere, but couldn't quite find it.

I had to start sorting out what the Bible truly said from the legends of the Jewish people about the patriarchs and also some notions about the law. I was surprised that the Bible does not forbid people from eating milk with meat. In reality that prohibition was an understanding that the rabbis obtained from an obscure verse that said, "Thou shalt not seethe a kid in its mother's milk."

It is not easy to unlearn things while learning, and my educational process was being impaired by a combination of my naivete and stubbornness.

Then there were the problems of poverty. February of 1954 was one of the coldest winters on record in the greater New York area. I had only a thin suit coat that was more appropriate to the month of July. Not only did I not have any money to buy a coat, but I wouldn't have known where to buy one. It was then I began to learn the meaning of petition for my life.

On a cold, snowy February day, I had to make the eighteen mile trip into New York City to serve as a volunteer at the American Board of Missions to the Jews. No person saw me when I was cold because I was careful to compose myself and warm up in the washroom. However, Miss Hilda Koser, one of the staff missionaries who had a children's class in Manhattan, approached me. In those days, missionaries called everybody "Mister" or "Miss" in respectful religious formality. She was very polite, saying, "Mr. Rosen, I hope you won't be offended if I bring a matter up to you, but one of the friends of our mission has died out in Michigan and his wife has sent us his clothes. I don't know if you need any clothes, but I brought them in today, and I was particularly thinking that this overcoat could fit you."

When I looked at that box of clothing, I didn't see how such a small woman could have carried that box in. The coat was almost new, a Hart Schaffner and Marx, much better than I could afford. There were also three winter suits and many shirts. Everything fitted me as though it had been tailored for me. God did answer prayer, except that I didn't remember praying. However, I was desperate and I must have prayed.

A few days later, I do remember praying. I had to turn in a typed paper, and my portable typewriter was at a repair shop. Although the charge was only $3.50, it might as well have been $3,500,000, because I didn't have it and would never have considered borrowing either a typewriter or money.

Benjamin Franklin's adage about neglect is true: "For want of the nail the shoe was lost; for want of a shoe the horse was lost; and for want of a horse the rider was lost." The horse was this particular paper, and I knew it. I prayed that I might get my typewriter.

I received very little mail and so I don't know why I felt led to reach my hand all the way back into the mailbox that day to pull out an envelope from the Public Service Company of Colorado containing a refund for my deposit on my gas and electricity. It must have been sitting there for a long time, as it was now February and the check was dated September. I got my five dollars; I got my typewriter; I got my paper done; I got an *A* on the paper; and God answered prayer.

It seemed that each week there was some answer to prayer, a prayer that I prayed for myself or a prayer that I prayed for someone else. For example, I needed work and a church. A man sought me out because he understood that I had experience in a sporting goods store. He told me that Sears and Roebuck needed someone in its sporting goods store, and I got the job. How could he have known that I had prayed for a job.

Then there were prayers where I petitioned for people to be saved and they were. It seemed as though each week there was some petition and some answer to prayer. My faith was being built up. I came to believe in petition, but I found that God didn't answer every prayer. I wasn't encouraged always by almost immediate answers to prayer. Instead I had found a deeper and abiding faith in which I was willing to ask God and trust Him about when He wanted to answer. He still blesses me with messages from that almost inaudible voice.

**Ronald J. Matlack**

# ~ 18 ~

# Twenty-four Hours a Day, Seven Days a Week

## Ronald J. Matlack

*Ronald J. Matlack is currently directing the RUN (Reaching Urban Neighborhoods) ministry of the Pocket Testament League, working in cities all along the East Coast. He was born in Camden, New Jersey, grew up on Long Island, and graduated with his wife, Hazel, from the first four-year class of Northeastern Bible College, the class of 1965. Their first child, Lisa, was born in the United States in 1967. Then the Matlacks spent sixteen years in church planting and radio work with headquarters in Trieste, Italy. Mr. Matlack was field director there for WEF Ministries for ten years. Two children were born there: Bradley in 1970 and Carla in 1972. In 1983, the Matlacks returned from Italy and became associated with the Pocket Testament League.*

My most memorable experience with God was not a single vision in the night nor a dramatic protection from an assassin's knife. It was sixteen years of helping me fulfill a vision of bringing local Christian radio to Italy. My wife and I went to Trieste, Italy, in 1967 to serve in church planting and radio ministry.

By the early 1970s turmoil had come to Italy, and our mission had to close our radio production and recording studios. All radio and television stations were controlled by the government.

As we closed down our work, the Lord gave us a strong desire and an urgent prayer: "Lord, someday open the door to radio for us again. Give us time on local radio stations within Italy." We would have settled for fifteen minutes a week.

By the mid 1970s, the Italian economy and political institutions were ridden with problems. The oil crunch created enormous difficulties for the economy. Inflation was out of control. There were rationing and strikes. Terrorism was rampant. Businessmen carried guns. There were constant bombings at airports and train stations.

Seizing the opportunity in this period of national confusion, a group of sharp politicians and businessmen planned a major assault against the Italian government's monopoly of the radio waves. Politicians who were not part of the ruling party were being excluded from the government-controlled radio and television and wanted their views to be heard. Big business saw potential for a vast market in publicity and increased radio and television sales. However, what these men did not realize was that although they were ungodly, God was working through them to answer missionaries' prayers.

Some businessmen constructed a small radio station. The day the station went on the air, the Italian police arrested everyone involved. The businessmen's plan was working. A court battle ensued. One of the best legal minds in all of Italy was hired to defend the businessmen. The trial was long and expensive, but victorious for the businessmen *and for us.*

All laws governing radio and television broadcasting in Italy were declared unconstitutional, including the law that gave the government the exclusive monopoly to broadcast. After having one of the most restrictive broadcasting laws in the world, Italy found itself with no broadcasting laws or controls.

However, no one expected what followed. No radio law meant anarchy on the air waves. The weak government was unable to write another law, and so for the following two years the radio waves were controlled by the Italian young people who grouped themselves together, built or bought cheap, low-powered transmitters and homemade antennas, pooled their turntables and tape decks from home, attached a microphone, and went on the air.

It was survival of the strongest. If one station could broadcast on a certain frequency with more power than another, the stronger station prevailed until someone with a more powerful transmitter took it away. Obviously, transmitter quality was poor. At times airports had to close because their radar was disturbed by some private radio station. The police were having the same problem with interference in their signals.

Soon after the law governing broadcasting had been declared unconstitutional, I was called to a meeting in the city of Modena. Back to the Bible Broadcasts was asking the question, "What now?" At that meeting, we made an important decision. We did not know where we would find staff or how we would produce programming, but together we would seek to fund and construct low-powered FM radio stations and place them with Christians throughout Italy. God was answering prayer; He was giving us the possibility to broadcast twenty-four hours a day, seven days a week!

This news quickly spread throughout the evangelical community in Italy. Everyone wanted a station in his own town or city. It was the beginning of a networking of many local Christian radio stations that would reach into every city street and country lane. The gospel would be preached in Italy as it had never been preached before.

I returned home from the meeting with good news and bad news. The good news was that we were going on the air. The bad news was that not one of us knew the first thing about the technical or production end of radio. We had a lot to learn in a hurry, and the only encouraging factor was that none of the secular private stations knew much about radio production either.

All kinds of radio signals were coming into our area. The Italian government was broadcasting on several frequencies, and every day more frequencies were being occupied by enthusiastic youth. Signals were coming in from foreign radio stations as well. We had to find a vacant frequency on the radio dial, and so I began to visit local stations to compile a list of frequencies. I found stations in the strangest places: in attics, in basements, in trucks parked on mountain tops. One station was in a teenage boy's bedroom. He had a small transmitter attached to an antenna on the roof of the apartment building in which he lived.

I soon realized that the only way I could find a vacant frequency was to take a portable radio to a mountain top and begin to search for a free spot on the dial, a process I had to repeat three times.

Shortly after the first time I found a frequency, I received a phone call from a technician "friend" I had met at another station. He was very interested to know how my search was going. I gave him the good news and the frequency on which we would be broadcasting. He too was very happy and opened his own station on that frequency two days later! So, for me it was back to the mountain top.

This time, I told no one in the city of the new frequency except the company that was building our transmitter. Two days later, the frequency number had already filtered back to the city and within a week another station was on that frequency. So again for me it was back to the mountain top.

Finding a frequency had become not only a technical struggle but also a spiritual battle. We daily had to seek God's strength to continue. Satan could not have the victory that he so desired.

My third mountain top search lasted two weeks before I found a small, vacant spot. When I called the technicians building the transmitter to let them know that I had a frequency, I did not give the numbers but instructed them to call me for the frequency setting when the transmitter was built.

One week later, we were on the air. We shouted, we sang, we praised the Lord.

That first transmitter was two hundred watts, attached to a twenty-foot antenna on a rooftop of a house three hundred feet up a hillside. Attached to the transmitter was a tape machine with pre-recorded messages.

In the years to follow, studios would be built, an antenna site high over the city would be leased, and a more powerful transmitter would be purchased, but none of the large and more elaborate equipment created as much excitement as that first transmitter and antenna. Christian radio was on the air. God had answered prayer! We had asked for fifteen minutes; He had given us twenty-four hours a day seven days a week.

Now that we were on the air, we had another obstacle: the anti-Christian government of the city from which we were broadcasting. It was one thing when a group of kids started a radio station. Everyone laughed and endured the kids. But when adults went on the air representing a mission organization that was teaching doctrines differing from the state religion, the city took notice.

We had informed the police by letter of our intentions. There was no law to stop us from broadcasting, but we could be arrested at will on some technicality or even have our residence visas cancelled.

A police car took up residence outside our front door. Friends and neighbors told of the questions they were being asked about us. To be under police scrutiny is scary. To be afraid may be unspiritual but we were afraid, not of being found out as there was nothing to find out. We were afraid of being closed down.

It was several weeks before the police came to talk to us, but the knock finally came at our door. There were a hundred questions that I answered as well as I could, only to be asked the same question in a different way. We were not being accused, but we were forced to defend who we were and what we were doing. The detective left that evening with kind words, and I was finally able to relax. I did not know where his visit would lead, but at least it was over.

A short time later our first studio was completed. We had been on the air several months when we decided to give a phone number over the air. In the following ten weeks we received over twelve thousand phone calls. These first calls were not reporting conversions but rather expressing satisfaction with the station. The typical caller said, "Thank you for your broadcasts." "Thank you that there is no profanity on your station." "Thank you that you are doing something positive for our community." We had the city's ear.

The radio team that God had put together was beautiful. Several American missionaries and many Italians were struggling together to glorify God. People from the community came to do community-centered programs. At times people from the government radio donated time. As we needed special technical help, there was a listener we could call upon. Back-to-the-Bible sent us programs in Italian.

Then a courageous young Italian businessman legally put his name and business behind the radio as the person responsible before the Italian government. This new believer gave hours and days of his time to see that the radio was as legally protected as possible and to prepare the station to meet any future government requirements. He was willing to give his time and money and to stake his reputation in order to provide Christian radio. Radio in our city would not have continued without him.

Once again, we were called before the chief detective of police investigating any political and potentially subversive activity. We went with mixed feelings. If we were forced off the air, it still would have been worth all the work. We had made great gains; doors had been opened; and many had heard the gospel for the first time.

The chief did not waste time. He told us that his wife listened to our station and he himself listened at times. His investigation completed, he knew our motives and objectives and liked what we were doing morally for the community, but he was most interested in us for another reason.

Because we were different from the other stations that used their positions to speak out strongly against the government, he could use us as a model of what the other stations should follow. We were convenient for him because he could cite us in saying that he was not against all private radio. He offered us 100 percent protection and gave us a private number that would bring immediate police response.

God had not only answered prayer by giving us radio, but He had also given us protection through the forces that would have arrested us for broadcasting just two short years before. How do you begin to thank God for that? Words seemed to be too small.

After sixteen years in Italy, I boarded a plane in September, 1983, to return to the States. As the plane became airborne, I looked down over our city. I could see north to the Alps and then south along the Italian peninsula. All that fell within my sight was covered with Christian radio. Twenty-four hours a day, seven days a week, a network of local Christian stations was covering Italy and spilling across the borders into neighboring countries.

All this is a testimony to the greatness of our God. He had heard the feeble prayers of His children and had answered in His strength and glory. Praise God!

**David A. Rupprecht**

# ~ 19 ~
# God's Work Through Sabbath Rest

## David A. Rupprecht

*David A. Rupprecht has been pastor of Budd Lake Union Chapel of Budd Lake, New Jersey, since 1970 when he was a new graduate of Northeastern Bible College. He was born May 16, 1947, on a farm in central New Jersey and grew up in a local Baptist church where he became a born-again Christian at the age of sixteen through the influence of youth leaders there.*

*In addition to his B.R.E. from Northeastern, he earned a Th.B. in 1971 there, and in 1978 an M.A. from New Brunswick Theological Seminary in New Brunswick, New Jersey, and a D.Min. from Westminster Theological Seminary of Philadelphia, Pennsylvania, in 1983.*

*In 1973 Dr. Rupprecht married Ruth Huslage, and they have two children: Kara, age eleven, and Kirk, age eight.*

*The Rupprechts have preached and practiced the philosophy of what they call "radical hospitality." In one of his publications Dr. Rupprecht described that concept: "The ministry of radical hospitality . . . is opening a Christian home, . . . a home where family members are consciously working at their relationships to the Lord God and to each other—to some one who has been torn emotionally or relationally by sin or by others so that he or she can see first hand the power of God to redeem, change and heal."*

*Dr. Rupprecht was founder and director of the Community Counseling Center of Budd Lake, 1981–1987, a member of the*

*Board of Directors of the Berachah Farm Group Home of Es-
tella, Pennsylvania, 1985–1987, and on the Shepherding Home
Committee of the Friendship Crisis Pregnancy Center of Morris-
town, New Jersey, in 1984. He was named Humanitarian of the
Year in 1979 by the Hackettstown, New Jersey, Chamber of Com-
merce.*

*He has written numerous magazine articles, given seminars,
radio and personal presentations, and published two books in
his special area:* Radical Hospitality *and* Radical Hospitality
Leader's Guide.

*For the past ten years he has taken active leadership in activi-
ties of the Northeastern Bible College Alumni Association, was
president of the Association in 1976–1978, and was named
Alumnus of the Year in 1983.*

---

By the spring of 1987 I had had it. It was time to send out
some resumes, maybe even leave the ministry all together. The
saying that I naively had laughed at over the years, "To work
with the saints above, that will be glory; but to work with the
saints below, that's another story," had moved from the realm of
head knowledge to the realm of experience.

Ours is a community church, I kept reminding the people. It's
not a Baptist church, or a charismatic church, or a Reformed
church; in fact, we have something to offer everyone. We must
co-exist in love, we must transcend the denominational divisions
that divide Christ's body, and endeavor to keep the unity of the
spirit in the bond of peace. But the spiritual egotists, those that
know just how the church should be and what the church should
believe, came and departed, leaving their wake of destruction.

Who am I? There was a time when I knew. How much easier
it would have been for our church to adhere to denominational
distinctives, to feel secure in an identity, but instead we are not
conservative enough for the conservatives and we are not pro-
gressive enough for the progressives. My heart was broken. All I

wanted was the unity of the body so that the world would know that God had sent his Son.

So began my spiritual journey into what would ultimately bring renewal to one who was burned out and exhausted. Seventeen years in my first parish was an absurdity in its own right. In our fast-paced, mobile, consumer-oriented, get-a-better-deal society, why was I still at this church? There must be something wrong with me. But where your investment is, so your heart will be also.

I arrived with nothing to a church described by the part-time pastor before me as "an impossible situation if seen through the eyes of men." The twenty-five-dollar-a-week salary did not include housing and I was pioneering in a modern era that knows little of pain and sacrifice amid a culture that wants it all now. I started from the bottom and left many shaking their heads at my foolhardy attempts. I remodeled a condemned bungalow, the first parsonage, then an old barn, and began to minister through an extended family. Alienation, the product of modern society, was overcome for many through the ministry of the healing household. What a glorious revelation! A new environment, new family models, a new start for the bruised reeds and dimly burning wicks of which Isaiah spoke! And so they came— battered wives, single parents, rebellious teens, the divorced that the other churches had rejected—some forty-five of them over the years to make their home with us, to bring their pain into our day-to-day existence.

I worked on academic degrees. My motives were mixed; partially it was to advance the kingdom, but subconsciously I wondered if I had to do it to prove something to myself or someone else. Publish my thesis, I was advised, and so I took vacation time to write and rewrite, eventually holding the finished product in my hand.

So it had been seventeen years of preaching, problems, sacrifice, study, doing the dirty work that no one else would do to keep things going, and often feeling stabbed in the back by someone with whom I had cried, had spent hours counseling, and for whom at times I had moved refrigerators and even paid the bills. Seventeen years and I was burned out, or at least close to the edge.

*Go to another church; leave the ministry* were the thoughts that raced through my head. Then the suggestion came from my God-given helpmeet, "Who don't you take a sabbatical?" For someone who hardly knew what it was to take a day off, an alien thought began to haunt me. The sabbatical year meant fields left unplowed, a statement of trust in a sovereign God every seven years. But this is the twentieth century; you can't do that and run a ministry. Or can you? Was I ten years overdue? My perceptions had become warped, my emotions frazzled, my creativity spent, a cumulative pain brought depression, and I knew I had begun to become what I swore I would never be—a preacher who had to say something, rather than a preacher who had something to say.

Three months off, no sermons, no problems or people with which to contend or deal. The thought was foreign and the questions many. What will I do? What will I find when I return? Will the church fall apart without me? Ambivalence became my thinking pattern! I can't go, but I can't stay like I am. Take the sabbatical.

## May 31, 1987

My final Sunday: I finish the series on the Tabernacle. The Elders call Ruth and me in front of the church, lay hands on us and pray, releasing us with tears for what our God desires. Ambivalence continues: love–hate relationship, fear yet apathy, disillusionment; I know it's the end of an era.

## June 1

My first day off the job, seclusion in a cabin in the Poconos, a week all by myself. But, no, it can't be true! The hot water heater is leaking all over the floor. Why me? Maybe God doesn't want me to do this. Maybe He's trying to tell me something. Off to the plumbing store for parts and some five hours later I mop the kitchen floor. Time for a bath; let's take another try at this rest thing.

I read John Perkin's *A Quiet Revolution* that week, rode my bike, started to learn to play the guitar. I waxed my pickup truck and was starting to become a human again, starting to get in touch with myself again, starting to get over feeling guilty that I was away.

### June 20

What an incredibly mixed-bag I have created for this first month! The week at the old seminary I wanted to get into something intellectually stimulating but ended up reading *The Worldly Evangelicals,* a book I bought at the seminary store. My brain was fried (the intellectual part of me would have to be put on hold a while longer). The memories that swirled in that library: past anxieties, the hours on my Master's thesis, for what I ask? Why return to the scene of the crime? Who am I?

### June 29

It's crazy, I know it is, but I'm on sabbatical. I can do what I want! My blue collar roots, my hands-on, do-it-yourself farm boy values have taken over. The old '65 LeMans and I are at Dad's farm in Pennsylvania. This is reality: a week stripping off the paint, layer after layer; stripper, sander, dirt, grit, exhaustion, sore muscles; but a part of my humanity, a part of my identity, a part of who I was. Unsophisticated, unpretentious, I'm not made for the showmanship needed for the ministry today. Can I be happy working in a garage again?

### July 6

Kennedy Airport—far from a favorite place, but we await the Icelandic evening flight to Luxembourg. Out of the blue, or out of the hand of a sovereign God, during my wrestling time of yes/no sabbatical, we received an invitation to go to Holland to do a seminar with Dutch communities on radical hospitality. A mixed reaction on my part: I've been there before, why do I want to go back to Europe? Radical hospitality—that's old hat— my head is somewhere else now—I'm into affordable housing for the soon-to-be-forgotten middle class. But my wife and the kids are anxious to go, so I'll do it for them. I don't want people to think I've deprived my kids.

A month of travel: visit missionary friends in Germany, drive through the Black Forest, tour the Dachau concentration camp, the Holocaust courses seen in real life, the train to the flat lands of Holland. A whirlwind weekend speaking through a translator followed by a surprise invitation later that week at the Dutch L'Abri—good for the sagging ego. Kara mistaken for a German fraulein by Korean tourists at Heidelberg Castle, Kirk leading us through the maze of the Luxembourg casemates, experiences making the children and Ruth happy.

## August 7

Back home and time to reflect; a sense of renewal has slowly crept back. A renewed vision for the ministry of the healing household was re-established by the positive responses of those at the weekend seminar and L'Abri. Perhaps I'm more European in my thinking than American; maybe I'm not crazy—it just might be the rest of the world. Europeans understand counter-culture better than American Christians do.

The question: Do I take another month? They said I could. Trudy called; she has a dresser for Kara so I'll run down and get it. People have been so good. The phone that I had begun to hate has hardly rung at all. Trudy unloads on me about the problems she had this summer; I handled it OK. I didn't walk away as if someone had stabbed me and I couldn't stop the bleeding. Maybe I am ready to go back, and September is certainly the most expedient time; it all begins then. I'm somewhat back to normal, back to my old self. Everything will be OK. I can hack it.

## August 22

Anxiety attacks these last three Sundays. I can't believe it. My jaw would get tight before when stressed out, but now my chest is tightened like a rubber band ready to snap. Never in my life have I had this. I can't go back, I don't want to go back. I'll send my wife back to teaching. Her old school promised they'd always make room for her. What will I do? I don't know, but I can't go back. I don't want to get up there again.

To the members of the congregation:
    I hereby submit my resignation as pastor effective 9/1/87.

What happened? I just had two and a half months off and I'm worse now than when I first left. Sabbatical? Is it Satan's last-ditch effort to blow things?

Prayer, faith, reassurance, rest—sabbatical rest. I need to get it into my head that I don't have to perform for the masses of Christendom. People will come and people will go; I don't have to please men, only God. I need to hold on to that, rest in that. Yes, the mind and emotions are somewhat better; I can focus and find my perspective better than before. Rest in the fact that God has given me a faithful remnant of committed believers. He calls me to serve not for the praise of men but for the Lord. The purpose of sabbatical was to learn a deeper trust. I must go back. God opened no other doors; the fleece was not given. So I reject the anxiety as from the evil one and press on toward the prize of the high calling of God.

The church was near capacity despite the Labor Day holiday weekend. The greetings were warm and the faces expectant. I stood in the pulpit preaching the lessons from Gideon's three hundred men, calling us to renewal and battle against the evil one. The Sunday dinner table was again full as we re-opened our home.

I remember the sociology professor talking about a cultural lag, when segments of the culture lag behind the rest of the culture, like the Amish. So, I too would experience a rest lag that would begin that first September Sunday back and has continued. A new era has begun, as I knew it would, but my emotions had God's time to heal. That cumulative pain that I carried was reduced, greatly replaced by a renewed sense that God was in control. I was touched with a fresh understanding that this was His ministry not mine, that He must do it, and that my job was to enter His rest and cease from my own labors. The great works of God are not always evidenced in works. They are as well evidenced in rest.